A God Worth Waiting For

Vaughn Aaron Foster, Sr.

Table of Contents

Acknowledgements

No song sung, sermon preached, book written, or life lived for or about God could have been so without the merciful intervention and inspiration of God who makes all things possible. I am eternally indebted to and thankful for the presence and grace of God the Father, Son and Spirit in my life and for the privilege of being used by God to pen the words found between the covers of this book.

There are so many who have touched my life and have played a major role in me becoming the man of God I am today. However, for this particular writing, there have been certain people who have been invaluable and without whom I do not believe this book could have come through me. I am privileged to acknowledge my gifted and amazing wife Lisa whose love and support has had no boundaries and has helped me to be both what and who I am. I also want to acknowledge our two sons, Vaughn and Elijah. I cannot adequately express how much they have been used by God to reveal who He is, who I am in Him and how much our relationship is and should be a mirrored image of what God shares with His children here on earth.

Also, I would like to thank the Rev. Dr. Roy Medley for his contribution to this writing. Along with thousands of others, I have been touched by his humble disposition, strong leadership and godly standards as displayed in his role as Executive Minister of ABC-USA. Next, I must recognize the Grace Baptist and Perfecting Saints Church, among whom this book was birthed. Also, I must acknowledge my pastor and friend, Doug Neavin, First Baptist Church and New Hope Fellowship Chapel of Steubenville, OH. Without your prayerful support and faithful friendship, the temptation to become weary in well doing would have prevented me from completing this labor of love.

I certainly must acknowledge my mother Carolyn Brown-Williams; my father-in-law and mother-in-law, The Rev. William A. Reeves, Sr. and Annie Reeves; three special women of God: The Rev. Lisa Harris, Roslyn Purnell and Melinda Brown, who have helped me remember what God has called me to do, why God called me to do it and to bring it to completion amid the overwhelming distractions of life and ministry. In addition to those already mentioned, there are several who were critical in getting this book from my laptop to publication: Joe Brown, Arnold Hamm, and The Revs. Joshua Smith and Pamela Bowers-Smith. Thank You!

It would also be appropriate for me to mention Michael and Djanaba Bateman whom I love as son and daughter and as friends. It's awesome to see how

God rarely places people in your lives to be blessed, who do not turn out to be among your greatest blessings!

Lastly, I want to acknowledge my bishop, Dr. Donald Hilliard, Jr. There is not a day that goes by that I am not soberly aware of the formative work that God performed in my life while under his tutelage – Thank you!

Forward
The Rev. Dr. A. Roy Medley

This book is for everyone who has grown weary in "the waiting room," questioning why God has not acted as we had hoped, prayed, or assumed.

Writing with a shepherd's heart, Pastor Foster addresses this issue knowing it is one of the most vexing faced by Christians in daily life. And with wisdom, he does so by sharing with us his own struggles in the waiting room and how he has experienced God's faithfulness and blessing, though not always in the manner he had anticipated.

He wisely reminds us that "so often we want deliverance and not development." In his sincere and loving manner, Rev. Foster offers encouragement to everyone who waits anxiously for God to act, instilling confidence in us as he helps us understand God's purpose of developing us into trusting disciples as we wait.

His treatment of the practice of prayer, petition and thanksgiving while in the waiting room is particularly insightful, as well as his warning against taking matters into our own hands "cloning God's promise."

Both new and mature Christians will find insights here that open their eyes to God's trustworthiness, a God worth waiting for.

Rev. Dr. A. Roy Medley
General Secretary
American Baptist Churches USA

Dedication

This book is dedicated to those
whose season is before them
Those whose time is still not at hand
It is dedicated to the people of God
who wait on Him
Seeking a word, wanting His will,
trying to understand

This book is dedicated to those
who have a call and even an anointing
But who find the silent wait for God
at times disappointing
This book is dedicated to those whose destiny
Still awaits its fulfilling
Those whose flesh grows tired
though their spirits remain willing

This book is dedicated to those desiring
like eagles to mount up and soar
Those, that amid life's discomforts,
Believe Yahweh to be the God worth waiting for

Section One

Who Are You Waiting For?

1

Is Your God Worth Waiting For?

Whenever God's people would look back in history to view confrontations between God and His adversaries they would probably recall Isaiah's account of Satan being kicked out of heaven (Isa. 14). Perhaps they would call to mind Dagon, with his head and hands broken off, lying prostrate before the Ark of the Covenant (1 Sam. 5:1-5). Surely, they would call to mind the series of plagues God used to twist Pharaoh's arm until he let the children of Israel go and the subsequent cost Pharaoh paid for changing his mind (Exod. Ch. 12-14).

They would also, undoubtedly, recall the day when Elijah told King Ahab, "Now summon the people from all over Israel to meet me on Mount Carmel. And bring the four hundred and fifty prophets of Baal and the four hundred prophets of Asherah, who eat at Jezebel's table" (1 Kings 18:19). This was to be the showdown of all showdowns. With complete and utter confidence in Yahweh, Elijah told the prophets that they were more in number and should be the first to call on their god to send fire from heaven. However, despite hours of crying, pleading, and self-mutilation these prophets could not get their god out of the dressing room. What had been ticketed as "The Fight of the Century" turned out to be a big "No Show"! While the King James Version of the Bible states that the prophets cried for Baal to hear (1 Kings 18:26), these prophets did not merely want a hearing; they wanted an answer. In Hebrew, both the cry of these prophets to Baal and the request of the prophet Elijah to God was that they would eye or heed, i.e. pay attention. In essence, the word means "to respond." Perhaps there would be other times when simply being heard would be appropriate, but for this day, an answer was needed. Yet, the scripture says, for the prophets who opposed Elijah "there was no voice." No one called aloud. No one cried back. There was no answer or response; and there was no one who hearkened or regarded. In today's English, no one paid them any mind at all. Baal didn't say a mumbl'n word. Was Baal musing? Was he working? Was he sleeping such a deep sleep that not even his prophets' denigrating and humiliating performance could awaken him? Perhaps he had indeed "gone aside." Whatever the case, it was clear that in waiting for their god to appear and act, these prophets had waited in vain.

Baal (which means lord or commander) was the god of the Phoenicians and Chaldeans. While God continually warned His people against idolatry, they always seemed to have an interest and sometimes an infatuation with the gods of other nations. In Joshua's farewell address, he commanded the people with this in mind: "Now fear the Lord and serve him with all faithfulness. Throw away the gods your forefathers worshiped beyond the River and in Egypt, and serve the Lord" (Josh. 24:14). Talk about godly counsel! Then, perhaps because people back then were like people today, he adds... "But if serving the Lord seems undesirable to you, then choose for yourselves this day whom you will serve, whether the gods your forefathers served beyond the River, or the gods of the Amorites, in whose land you are living. But as for me and my household, we will serve the Lord" (Josh. 24:15). The people insisted that they would also serve the Lord. However, never would Joshua's words be truer. Time after time, the people forsook the Lord and served foreign gods. In return, time after time, the Lord brought disaster on them and made an end of them, after he had been good to them (24:20). Today, like Israel and Judah, God's people seem to live by the well known rephrasing of St. Ambrose's words to Augustine, "When in Rome, do as the Romans do..."

When Joshua says, "As for me and my house ..." he is not simply informing the people of his personal decision to follow Yahweh. He is recommending that the people trust and serve the same God he has come to trust and is committed to serve. This is not a new concept. If we take a close look at the Psalms, we find in more than a few that David, like Joshua, begins by testifying of God's faithfulness. However, also like Joshua, he encourages the reader to (or expects the reader to) benefit from his experience. For instance, in Psalm 27, David wrote, "I had fainted, unless I had believed to see the goodness of the Lord in the land of the living" (Ps. 27:13 KJV). Clearly, each of us has faced periods in life when we grew tired and fainting was a realistic option. David says when he was in this situation he believed or trusted that he would see the goodness of the Lord. In other words, David is saying that amid his trouble, persecution, trials and tribulations, it was his faith that the Lord was worth waiting for that enabled him to hang on and not faint. He then encourages the reader to do what he did: "Wait on the Lord: be of good courage, and he shall strengthen thine heart: wait, I say, on the Lord" (Ps. 27:14). David does not merely encourage us to wait; he encourages us to wait on Yahweh. Believe it or not, it does matter who you wait for. They that wait on false gods find themselves disappointed. However, "those who hope in [expect or wait on] the *Lord* will renew their strength. They will soar on wings like eagles; they will run and not grow weary, they will walk and not be faint" (Isa. 40:31).

One afternoon, while making hospital visits I stopped in several rooms to pray for people I did not know. (Our relatives, friends and church members are not the only people in need of prayer.) When I offered to pray for one woman she responded, "Sure, I'll accept prayer from anyone." If we are to take this woman's statement literally, she would accept prayer from a Christian, Muslim, Buddhist, or Satanist. Like this woman, regrettably, many of our Sunday church attendees have no preference from where their "blessing" comes. After getting "inspired" by the choir and twenty minutes of soul-stirring but, unfortunately, not life-altering preaching they go home and call a psychic for counsel. So many of our faithful church members, after receiving a thought provoking message consisting of three points and a poem (or hymn), never cease to "knock on wood" after counting their blessings. We call Jesus "Savior," but who or what is our lord? We worship Yahweh and we worship Baal. How long will we go "limping with two different opinions?" When will we dethrone the Baal in our lives so that Yahweh, so that Jesus, may be Lord indeed? Who or what is your god and is your god worth waiting for?

Often in scripture, the word Baalim appears rather than Baal. Baalim is the plural form of Baal. There was not simply one "lord" but several "lords." In the same sense, in both Christian and non-Christian homes it seems as though everyone has a Baal. We may never fashion a god out of wood or metal and call it Baal but we still have tangible gods that we worship every day — tangible gods such as husbands, wives, children, boyfriends and girlfriends. We worship tangible gods such as automobiles and houses, electronic devices and money. Some of us worship intangible gods such as sleep and work. For some, even sex is a god. Still others worship Baal in the person who drives the Mercedes

Benz or Hummer to work, parks by the door and sits in the big office across from our cubicle. This Baal is the person who signs our pay checks or approves our raises. Most of us would never call this person Baal but Paul wrote, "Don't you know that when you offer yourselves to someone to obey him as slaves, you are slaves to the one whom you obey — whether you are slaves to sin, which leads to death, or to obedience, which leads to righteousness" (Rom. 6:16 RV)?

Why would I say Baal instead of supervisor or manager? Too often, the supervisor or manager on our jobs holds more authority over our lives than our children, our spouses, the pastor, than even God. It is frightening how a person who does not know God, does not want to know God and could not care less about what we think about God, can so easily control the time we spend in the presence of God. Men, women, and even teens, miss revivals, Bible studies and Sunday services because they willingly submit to a person who does not have their spiritual well-being in mind.

Did I say, "They?" *We* willingly submit to a person who does not have our spiritual well-being in mind. Although it may have begun as forced over-time, after a while our desire to be impressive and our hunger to be affirmed by those in authority cause us to yield ourselves as slaves. We forget that apart from God's divine plan for our being there, it is just a job. Consequently, we lose intimacy with our spouses, our children barely know us, our friendships are neglected, our ministry outside of work is starved and our relationship with God begins to wither.

For many Christians, Baal is the TV listing (or menu) that instructs us when we can do the things God has called us to do. We have gotten used to not watching much television on Wednesday nights because it is Bible Study night. However, let there be a request for our attendance on an additional night. "Well, uh, well, uh, I would love to go with you to the revival, but tonight is Family Night." Then, all night while our God-given family is eating dinner, playing board games and enjoying one another's company, we are watching our favorite TV families.

If it sounds like I am preaching, just know that even preachers need to hear a good sermon. We have enough televisions in our home for everyone to watch what he or she wants at the same time. I still remember growing up with one television in the house. It only got about four stations and that was if the shirt hanger replacing the broken antenna was positioned properly. Now we can watch ESPN, HGTV, Cartoon Network and PBS all at the same time. Lord, help us!

What am I trying to say? When God said, "You shall have no other gods before me" (Exod. 20:3), those words were not merely contextual and they did not come with an expiration date. The commandments of old are to be taken as seriously today as when God first spoke them to Moses. He meant that we shall have no other gods before Him — tangible or intangible, in priority or presence. God should be our number one priority. Nothing should have precedence over God. There should be no person, no occupation, no habit or hobby that has greater influence over our lives than God.

Although I have mentioned a few of the gods who sometimes rule and reign in our lives, only you and God know which gods are alive, well and seated on the throne of *your* life. To identify these gods, examine your time, your talent and your treasure. Who gets the majority of your time? The God-given abilities given to you are most often used on whom? Then there is that old detective saying: "Follow the money!" We spend money on the people and things we cherish most. Yet, as referenced in Luke 12:21, how rich are we toward God? I hesitate to say it but some families, generation after generation, have poured money into a church building. As a result, it does not matter what God, the pastor, or anyone else says or does, the only way to separate them from that church is by casket and pallbearers. Sometimes this is a God-honoring commitment. At other times, this is "temple worship;" not worship in the temple but the worship of the temple. However, one day, as Jesus told the disciples concerning the Jerusalem temple, "Do you see all these things?" he asked. "I tell you the truth, not one stone here will be left on another; every one will be thrown down" (Matt. 24:2).

Let me say one more thing on this matter. Do not let it surprise or discourage you when you dethrone one god and suddenly find another in its place. Everyday we need to ask the Lord, "Search me, O God, and know my heart; test me and know my anxious thoughts. See if there is any offensive way in me, and lead me in the way everlasting" (Ps. 139:23-

24). We serve a merciful God who, despite His hatred and lack of tolerance for the idols in our lives, loves us and wants us free to love Him, worship Him and fulfill His divine plan for our lives.

2

Luck Be A Lady

For many, the god in whom they trust and for whom they wait has been described in Frank Sinatra's song, *Luck Be a Lady*. In this 1960 classic Sinatra sings,

> *They call you Lady Luck but there is room for doubt.*
> *At times you have a very un-lady-like way of running out.*
> *You're on a date with me, the pickins have been lush*
> *and yet before the evening is over you might give me the brush.*
> *You might forget your manners you might refuse to stay.*
> *So the best I can do is pray ... Luck be a lady, Luck be a lady,*

Luck if you've ever been a lady ... Luck be a lady tonight.

Albeit unstable and unreliable, both Christians and non-Christians, repeatedly place their faith in something called luck. Daily it seems to rain pennies from heaven, until, at the most crucial of times luck runs out. Although the yields from the last few scratch offs were moderately lush, after purchasing forty dollars worth of lottery tickets in hopes of hitting the seventy-million dollar jackpot, luck gives them the brush. Instead of abandoning this god who leaves them feeling insecure and without peace, they go to the next venture with the prayer, "Luck be a lady tonight, Luck be a lady tonight. Luck if you've ever been a lady to begin with, Luck be a lady tonight."

Far too often we do what we have always done and expect that "one day my ship is gonna come in." Well, if Lady Luck is the captain of that ship, it has faced the same fate as the Titanic and we had better seek another mode of transportation and blessing.

One mild May afternoon I stopped at a convenience store to purchase pumpkin seeds. While it is common knowledge that I have an unshakable affinity for David Sunflower Seeds, every now and then, I crave pumpkin seeds. I searched and searched the car fearing that I may have dropped my wallet. It was nowhere in sight. While I slowly, carefully and systematically searched the car in hopes that I was not losing my mind and that I would not have to do the Motor Vehicle thing again, a woman pulled up next to me. She sat in the car for an unusual amount of time so I glanced over to see if I had something to do with her lingering. There she was going through a book that at a distance could easily be mistaken for a book of crossword puzzles. I knew better. Every now and then, I would take a casual glance in her direction to see if my suspicions could be verified. She continued to turn through the pages of the book and it was as though God Himself said, "She's looking for her lucky number." If this scene were not so sad it would be hysterical. She finally left the car and went into the store, and then I lost her. From the moment I saw her open that book I knew what she was up to and yet, as a person driving past an accident, my journey was not to be complete until I saw her at the machine. Although she did not go directly to the machine, she did go and there she purchased her ticket(s). I wanted so badly to interview her for this book but I got a revelation: my wallet was under the driver's seat. I got out of the car to get it and by the time I lifted my head she was pulling off.

This chain of events was not an accident and, God knows, it was not a lucky coincidence! Let me explain what I saw beyond what I saw. I saw a middle-aged woman on her last hope. I am not sure if she was married or had children but she appeared to be one with various bills and a desire for a better life. Perhaps she had a mortgage, a child in college, had been divorced from her husband and was handling life alone. There was no joy on her face as she searched the magazine. Instead, I sensed, perhaps, a bit of desperation. I tried not to stare, not simply because it was impolite but because I felt that my staring might embarrass her. Embarrassed or not she had things that needed to be taken care of and if she was ever to have all that she desired in life, Luck had to be a lady that night. However, I do not think Luck was a lady and this woman, if statistics prove true, is still trusting in a god who is not worth waiting for.

It is truly tragic to consider how many people have faith that despite the enormous odds, they will win a big payoff in a state's lottery drawing or a trip to Las Vegas or Atlantic City. As many would imagine, Focus on the Family (FOTF) is opposed to legalized-gambling. Although there are a number of extremely valid reasons to oppose gambling, a few of the more compelling found on the FOTF website are the following:

> Gambling is driven by and subsists on greed. For this reason, the activity is morally bankrupt from its very foundation. Gambling is also an activity which exploits the vulnerable — the young, the old, and those susceptible to addictive behaviors. Further, gambling entices the financially disadvantaged classes with the unrealistic hope of escape from poverty through instant riches, thus ultimately worsening the plight of our poorest citizens. Also, gambling undermines the work ethic. It is based on the premise of something for nothing, a concept that sanctions idleness rather than industriousness, slothfulness instead of initiative (http://www.family.org/socialissues/A000001124.cfm).

Many have written of the ills of gambling and the goal of this writing is not to add to the wealth of available information on the topic. In fact, most of the people I know who gamble via daily lotteries, etc. appear to be less motivated by greed than by a desperate attempt to lay hold of a better life. Perhaps this is what makes one of the sentences from the above quote so powerful: "gambling entices the financially disadvantaged classes with the unrealistic hope of escape from poverty through instant riches, thus ultimately worsening the plight of our poorest citizens."

While vacationing in Puerto Rico, my wife and I walked past a hotel that had a casino on the first level. I was determined to take a peak inside. One morning we walked inside and looked around. There were not many people there at 10:00 or 11:00 in the morning, but those who were there were a sight to see. People of varied ages (but the clear majority were senior citizens) sat at slot machines and, one pull after another, looked for their way of life to change. What was most shocking was that when bells went off indicating that the last pull was a winning pull, the players simply kept putting in coins and pulling again. There was no dancing, no shouting, and no celebration. In fact, there was no change in demeanor at all. It was as if the players were hypnotized or zombies. However, this scene was scarier than any horror film we had ever seen and our hearts broke.

In Greek, the word for faith, pistis, not only means to trust, it also means to entrust. When we have faith that Lady Luck is going to come through for us, we entrust to her our time, our resources, and our future. However, such trust for the provisions we need and for abundant blessings should not be placed in a "get rich quick scheme," working like a dog, or some unpredictable concept called Luck. Our faith, our trust, should be reserved for God. Proverbs chapter three puts it this way ...

> Trust in the Lord with all your heart and lean not on your own understanding; in all your ways acknowledge him, and he will make your paths straight. Honor the Lord with your wealth, with the firstfruits of all your crops; then your barns will be filled to overflowing, and your vats will brim over with new wine (Prov. 3:5-6, 9-10).

Some years ago, Sun America had a number of television commercials describing unusual circumstances where persons have found valuable things in unlikely places. In one of the commercials a person found an original copy of The Declaration of Independence behind a garage sale painting. The commercials for this financial investment company ended by asking the viewers how they planned to fund their future. In essence, the commercials ask, "Can Lady Luck be entrusted with your future?" As you long for, await and even seek a future that is brighter than the sun, can Lady Luck be entrusted with *your* future?

Section Two

A God Worth Waiting For

3

The Identity of God: Sovereign

Perhaps it seems strange that I chose to spend the first two chapters of this book pointing out some of the gods we have set up in our lives and unmasking them for the powerless bondage producing entities they are. Nevertheless, this is the very thing that Elijah did when he wanted to dethrone Baal and call the people back to a lively trust in God.

Still, it occurs to me that beyond addressing the flaws in false gods, it is impossible to speak about a God worth waiting for without saying a word about the identity of the true God who is worthy of our worship and our waiting. While there have been conversations, conferences and debates regarding who God is and to what degree God interacts with us, for the most part, I am a traditionalist at heart. I agree with the statement of belief articulated at the Council of Nicea in 325 AD:

> I believe in one God, the Father Almighty, maker of all things visible and invisible; and in one Lord Jesus Christ, the Son of God, the only-begotten of his Father, of the substance of the Father, God of God, Light of Light, very God of very God, begotten, not made, being of one substance with the Father. By whom all things were made, both which be in heaven and in earth.

If all of this sounds deep, well, it can be. For now, let us just say that, the God about whom I write is not "the Big Guy in the sky" or "The Man upstairs." Neither is God our "Cosmic Bellhop" who exists solely to be at our beck and call or our Genie who when rubbed with praise and worship will grant our every wish. No, this God is sovereign.

So often, Christians view God as that wonderful, yet perpetually tardy, saint who can never seem to be ready on Sunday morning. The night before, you make it unequivocally clear that you will be outside this person's home at 9:00 AM. At 9:00, this beloved child of God is not outside. You blow the horn — No response. Blowing the horn every five minutes: 9:05, 9:10 9:15, still, there is no response. Finally, with steam coming from under your hood and out of your ears you tear off leaving rubber marks in the street as a sign that you had been there. You finally arrive for Sunday school late, disheveled and irritated. After

Sunday School, that wonderful King's kid whom you left behind comes up to you looking like he just stepped out of a fashion magazine. As you await an explanation, an apology, a request for forgiveness, he says, "Praise the Lord! It's good to see you! Why did you leave me this morning? I heard you blowing but when I got outside you were gone. But that's all right. My cousin was running late and came by and got me." Albeit in a normal situation, perhaps this less than considerate Christian should have been left, we cannot apply the same standard to God.

It is crucial that we understand that God is indeed sovereign. If God decides that He would rather skip Sunday school and church too, we would do well to sit and wait. What a hilarious concept... rush off and leave God because God is not where we expected Him to be when we expected Him to be there and get to where we are supposed to go *with* Him by ourselves. I guess it is kind of like going to pick up your sister for her birthday party and because she takes too long, you leave and go to the party without her. As absurd as this sounds, more often than we would care to admit, when God does not move when we expect, in the way we expect, we attempt to seize the reigns of life and try to bronco-ride life until it submits to us. This type of thinking dethrones God and places us as kings and queens of our own lives.

In one of my favorite movies, *Staying Alive*, there is a scene where the dancers are rehearsing for a big production. John Travolta and Cynthia Rhodes stand and watch the star of the scene unable to perform a crucial part of the routine to the level expected by the director. John Travolta seizes the opportunity to step in and take over the lead. Not so with us! Not only is God the star of the show, God is the show. There is no one who can take His place. There is none who is His equal. As stated in Daryl Coley's song *Sovereign* written by Carol Antrom, "... God is sovereign. He can do whatever He wants to do... when He wants to... how He wants to because He's sovereign. God is God."

Toward the end of 2004, God made it clear that the time had come for my family and me to leave Grace Baptist Church. I had served as the pastor of the small but strong congregation for more than seven years and no matter what circumstance or situation beckoned me elsewhere, I refused to move unless or until God said "Move." In October of that year I announced to the congregation that God was saying, "Move." God did not tell me where we were to move, or how things were supposed to line up once we did move. As we attempted to sell our home, things progressed quickly and then they slowed to a crawl. As we sought a new home things moved quickly and then slowed to a crawl. It seemed every time we heard God say do something and tried to do it we had to toss out our own timetable and wait for God to bring what He said to pass. As we consider the identity of this God, for whom we wait, perhaps it is best to begin with His sovereignty.

What we had scheduled, planned and expected to take one month took more than six. Living in my mother's home and sleeping in her basement was something for which God had prepared us. However, what we thought was to be a minor layover turned out to be so much more. I am convinced that if I have to be in a waiting room, a great person to be there with is my mother. Through every delay, through every change, despite the varied obstacles and hindrances, she was unmoved and recognized God in both the minor and major aspects of it all. As always, my in-laws were also there encouraging and supporting us spiritually, emotionally and financially. Still, with the majority of our things in storage, Billie Holiday's words were oh so relevant: "Mama may have, Papa may have but God bless the child that's got his own." The truth is, God was blessing but we wanted more than a blessing. We wanted what He had promised — we wanted our own.

The sovereignty of God looks good and feels great when exercised over our situation or despite our enemy's intentions. Still when this same sovereignty alters our plans and programs and, in reality, alters us, it does not feel good at all. The apostle Paul wrote, "And we know that in all things God works for the good of those who love him, who have been called according to his purpose" (Rom. 8:28). Still, what we sometimes *feel* is better articulated by what Collin Raye wrote in his song *What I Need*, "I knew all the answers, the way my life should go. And when I used to say my prayers, I would tell God so. It seemed He wasn't listening, I thought He didn't care. But lookin' back it's plain to see He was always there" (Can't Turn Back, 2001). When God exercises His sovereignty over our lives it sometimes seems as though He doesn't hear us or care until we "look back."

The sovereignty of God not only means God has the *right* to do what He wants, it also means God has the *ability* to do what He wants. Elijah could expect God to respond to his request for fire from heaven because he knew that God was sovereign over every element required to bring about such a miracle. I will go further. Even if Baal could bring forth fire, because God is sovereign over all, on that day, Baal would not have been able to produce a spark. What am I saying? While any power attributed to Baal was as a result of superstition, the devil does have power. Nevertheless, because God is sovereign, "what He opens no one can shut, and what He shuts no one can open" (Rev. 3:7b).

In the Gospel of John Chapter 11, Mary and Martha were mourning the death of their brother Lazarus. Like many of us, they were able to predict what would have happened if things had gone the way they prayed. Upon Jesus' arrival, Martha said, "If you had been here, my brother would not have died" (v.21). We pray, "Lord, if only you had answered our prayer earlier... If only you had come when we called or given us what we asked for when we asked for it ..." However, the sovereignty of God means that even when God is too late, God is right on time. When the doctors have done all they can do, the undertakers have finished their work and the mourners have returned home, Yahweh is the type of God who asks, "Where have you laid him?" The same God, who sent fire at the request of Elijah, parted the Red Sea for Moses and the Israelites, and quieted raging storms for the disciples, can raise that which has died out of season and give it new life, because He is sovereign.

However trite, it is nevertheless true, God is able! It is possible to hear something so much that in addition to losing its novelty, the saying can lose its power. God can! When we realize that a promise is only as good as the ability of the one who makes it to perform it, we will become more discriminating about where we place our trust. With so many things in this world offering peace, joy, prosperity, wholeness, etc. we need to discern who is really able to follow up words with actions.

When Elijah called for the contest on Mt. Carmel with the prophets of Baal and Asherah he was not only saying their gods would not answer, he was saying they could not answer. The writer of Psalm 115, in comparing Yahweh to other gods, affirms Yahweh as the God who can and the others as gods who cannot:

Why do the nations say, "Where is their God?" Our God is in heaven; he does whatever pleases him. But their idols are silver and gold, made by the hands of men. They have mouths, but cannot speak, eyes, but they cannot see; they have ears, but cannot hear, noses, but they cannot smell; they have hands, but cannot feel, feet, but they cannot walk; nor can they utter a sound with their throats. Those who make them will be like

41

them, and so will all who trust in them (Ps. 115:2-8).

While other gods are unable to speak, see or act, Yahweh is able to perform what He declares. In fact, He told Jeremiah, "... for I will watch over My word to perform it" (Jer 1:12 MKJV). God can do what God says and watches over what He says until it is done!

In both Hebrew and Greek, a person's name was directly tied to who a person was and not simply what he or she was called. When Jesus told the disciples, "And whatsoever ye shall ask in my name, that will I do, that the Father may be glorified in the Son" (John 14:13 RV), he was in essence saying, "Whatever you ask in my personhood, my authority, on my behalf with my approval; whatever you ask that I would ask as if I am asking, I will do it." Such a promise can only be made by one who is a lunatic, liar or Sovereign Lord. Jesus is Lord and is in deed sovereign!

Sovereignty is one of God's most renowned attributes, especially for those who wait. Still, He is so much more! When questioned concerning His identity, Yahweh responded to Moses with the simple words, "I AM that I AM" (Exod. 3:14). This is to say, "I am who I am" or "I am He who exists." Scholars and Bible students have interpreted these words in so many ways it is often difficult to differentiate who God says He is from who we say He is.

In Exodus 17:15, God is referred to as Jehovah-Nissi, "The Lord my banner." When Abram was prepared to put everything on the line and even offer up the son of promise, Isaac, he found Yahweh to be his provider. "And Abraham called the name of that place Jehovah–Jireh: as it is said to this day, in the mount of the Lord it shall be provided" (Gen. 22:14 RV). Gideon, the recipient of an unanticipated visit from God that did not kill him as he expected it would, knew God as Jehovah-Shalom, the Lord is Peace (Judg. 6:24).

From Genesis to Revelation we learn about who God is. Yet, like those found throughout scripture, God calls us to enter into situations where our intimate interaction with Him will reveal a part of His character and nature that we may otherwise never truly know. The scriptures and so many who have believed them teach us about God. In addition, God, wanting us to go beyond knowing *about* Him to *knowing* Him, calls each of us to not only hear, but also to "taste and see." God wants us to experience for ourselves who He is, and what He is willing to do for those who will wait for Him.

4

The Trust Factor

Perhaps the greatest blessing of having children is to watch them in diverse situations and see how their response to life often mirrors our own. From the day our first son was born, my wife and I realized that the concept of waiting was not one that he would easily grasp. Whereas he was amazingly patient with diaper changes, when it came to eating, he did not want to wait. The slightest delay in getting him the food he desired caused that little baby to produce the largest disturbance. I am quite certain he could be heard across the street, if not down the block. Every now and then life causes us to do a "patience check." We get caught in traffic; a check we are waiting to receive in the mail doesn't show up when we expect it; we go to pick up someone and the person is not ready - life presents us with a variety of "patience checks." The funny thing is, because we handle the situation well, we believe we are patient. However, we got caught in traffic on our way to a job we did not want to perform. We expected a check on Monday but were paid from our job the previous Friday and had plenty of money in the bank. We went to pick up someone who was not ready but did not mind the wait because she wanted to buy us lunch. It is so easy to be patient about some things or in some situations and far more difficult to be patient about others. If we were broke and the check did not come we would all but go to the post office looking for it. If we were caught in traffic on the way to the movies, we would just about lose our minds. If we went to pick someone up for church and had to wait, only God's grace would keep him or her from having to take a taxi.

As our eldest son, Vaughn, got older and began to walk and talk, I noticed the strangest thing about him. He was ecstatic about the word "Yes." "No" was disheartening but pretty much ended the subject. However, the word "wait" was simply not the word to use. I can remember the many times when he misunderstood what I meant by "wait." "Juice, please?" he'd ask. "Yes, wait a minute." I'd reply. However, something always got lost in the translation. He did not understand me to say wait and I will get it in a moment. He understood me to say, "Wait until I finish my sentence and ask again." Other times he misinterpreted what I said completely and thought I said, "Wait until you get tired of waiting and then get it yourself." It is enough to make a person scream until we realize that at age 30, 40, or 60 we are no different.

If God says, "Wait," we wait until we are sure He said wait and then we ask again; or, we wait until we feel we cannot wait any longer and then attempt to do it ourselves. As our children grow to know us and trust us, their need for an instant response or to do things on their own diminishes. They begin to understand that wait does not mean no and it does not mean do it yourself. They begin to understand that wait means that I have heard your request, I have approved your request and I will grant your request at the proper time. It is only through knowing and trusting us as parents that our children come to this conclusion. Simultaneously, it is only through knowing God and trusting God that we wait on God.

I remember preaching a revival at my father-in-law's church. The theme was "Come Back to Your First Love." On one particular night, I was preaching, God was moving and then it happened! I got an amazing revelation: "We (pastors and preachers) are calling people back to a first love when many have not had an initial encounter." Sure, they had accepted Christ, but they really had not had an encounter with God that redefined who they were and the very course of their lives — a testimony.

Paul wrote to the church at Rome, "Everyone who calls on the name of the Lord will be saved. How, then, can they call on the one they have not believed in? And how can they believe in the one of whom they have not heard? And how can they hear without someone preaching to them" (Rom. 10:13-14)? The thing sought is salvation (in Greek it also means deliverance, protection, healing or preservation). However, Paul shows us that a person does not just receive salvation. There is a chain of events. First, God sends a person to preach the Gospel (the good news regarding Jesus Christ). Secondly, the preacher preaches the Gospel. Thirdly, the Gospel is heard. Fourthly, the Gospel is believed. Lastly, the hearer calls on the name of Christ and is saved, delivered, healed, etc. The same process that takes place for a person to be saved by God must also take place for a person to wait on God. A person calls on the name of Christ and a person waits on Christ because of the Trust Factor. "But how are men to **call** upon Him in whom they have not believed?" "But how are men to **wait** upon Him in whom they have not believed?" Can it truly be expected for a person to wait on someone who they know little about or have not come to trust? While possible, it is not probable.

Before I got my driver's license, one of my cousins used to allow me to shift the gears as he steered and operated the gas, brake and clutch pedals (not recommended for you at home). Needless to say, I learned to drive cars that had manual transmissions faster than I would have without that experience. Start somewhere! The key difference is instead of working up to the point where you are completely in control; you are trusting to the point where you will allow God to be completely in control.

I cannot state this next point more emphatically. Trust is a choice! I recall having a heated debate with a friend who was tempted to make a bad decision. This is not a judgment call. He had the opportunity to state the facts truthfully and without deception and trust God with the outcome, or to misrepresent the facts (i.e. lie) and get a "better" outcome. I recall him saying it was easier for me to trust God because of my experiences. As you examine the level in which you trust God, let me encourage you with the same thoughts I sought to encourage him, "You have to start somewhere!" You may not have years of trusting and depending on God under your belt. However, if you trust God for healing when you have a cold, it will be that much easier to trust him for healing if the doctor says you have something far worse. If you trust God with a dime of each dollar, as your finances increase, it will be easier to trust God with ten dollars of one-hundred or one-hundred of a thousand.

From the time we begin to stand and try to walk, something in us says we can do it on our own. It used to amaze me to watch our youngest son Elijah. If I fixed the bottle, no problem, but I dared not hold it while he drank. As soon as the bottle was prepared and within arms reach, he would snatch it and begin to drink. If Lisa tried to feed him and paused a bit too long, he would make every attempt to feed himself. At three, things are different – sometimes. He no longer needs help eating or drinking and does not mind some minor interference with holding a heavy glass or cutting his waffles. However, he is often far less cooperative when his brother tries to help him do new things. Sound familiar? If we have a need and God takes too long we will beg, borrow or steal in order to meet the need. All the while, there is a faint voice echoing in our minds and hearts asking, "Don't you trust me? Why don't you trust me?" We can attempt to fix our problems, provide for our own needs, get vengeance (or justice) for ourselves when we are wronged or we can hear God saying, "Be still, and know that I am God" (Ps. 46:10a)! As I watch our sons together I notice Vaughn ready and willing to help and Elijah more willing to receive some assistance and to trust his brother to aid him on the road to independence. God really does not want to do everything for us. God wants us to mature. At the same time, just like a loving parent or older sibling, God stands ready to assist when we need Him. Although it may be difficult, we must choose to trust that God knows when to step in and when we have matured enough to handle the situation. Trust is a choice!

5

Faith Comes By Hearing

How does a woman come to trust, to have faith in a God she has never trusted before? How does a man rely on a God he has never relied on before? Although we love Louisa M.R. Stead's song "'Tis so Sweet to Trust in Jesus," the truth is that while it is sweet to know that we *can* trust in Jesus and take Him at His word, it is not always easy or pleasurable to do so. The Bible says that we begin to trust Jesus by hearing the preacher preach, by hearing someone's testimony, by hearing a still small voice speak to our hearts because "Now faith is being sure of what we hope for and certain of what we do not see" (Heb. 11:1). The word used for faith in this text, *pistis*, in addition to the aforementioned definitions, at its core, means "persuasion." It is by hearing the word of God that we become persuaded.

Both the scriptures we read and the songs that have been written based on those scriptures build our faith and persuade us of the character and ability of God. In other words, faith comes when we believe the reports of others as to who God is and what God can do.

Matthew and Luke recorded that Jesus was known as a friend of tax collectors and sinners (Matt. 11:19 & Luke 7:34). John recorded Jesus' words "Greater love has no one than this, that he lay down his life for his friends" (John 15:13). Presumably having himself been persuaded, by scripture and personal experience, the hymnist Johnson Oatman, Jr. wrote, "There's not a friend like the lowly Jesus" (*No not One*, 1895). The writer of the book of Hebrews wrote that Jesus said, "Never will I leave you; never will I forsake you" (Heb. 13:5). Perhaps, based on these very words, an unknown nineteenth century hymn writer wrote "Never Alone." Despite whatever trials this writer may have been facing, no matter what tragedies had been confronted or obstacles overcome, he or she was persuaded of God's presence.

The scriptures introduce us to God as a relational God. We are encouraged to enter into and maintain a relationship with this God. While an intimate relationship with Him is of paramount importance, there are times when faith in who God is and what God can do seems to supersede our relationship with Him. Throughout scripture, we find those without covenantal relationships with God receive answers to their petitions because they have become persuaded by what they have heard. Perhaps you remember the Canaanite woman in Matthew 15 who came to Jesus because her little girl was demon-possessed. Jesus appeared unmoved by the magnitude of her plight, her shouting and her worship. In fact, Jesus told her, "It is not right to take the children's bread and throw it to the puppies" (v. 26 ISV). Her response moved him. She said, "Yes, Lord. But even the puppies eat the crumbs that fall from their masters' tables" (v. 27 ISV). To that statement Jesus replied, "O woman, your faith is great! Let it be done for you as you want...and that very hour her daughter was healed" (v.28 ISV).

Prior to trusting God with all of our lives, if we believe the reports that God is a healer, deliverer and way maker and trust Him with our problems, God may very well act — although He is by no means obligated to do anything for us at all. While it is often tempting to view worship as the central means to access God, worship alone is not enough. Hebrews 11:6 reads, "And without faith it is impossible to please God, because anyone who comes to him must believe that he exists and that he rewards those who earnestly seek him." Neither the Canaanite woman's desperation nor her worship got Jesus' attention. However, her faith in His identity and ability got her prayer answered! This woman said, in essence, "Lord, that's not a problem at all, let the children have the bread; my problem can be handled by just a few crumbs."

Faith always begins with hearing. I heard, despite my horrible performance in high school, that God could help me to succeed in college. I believed it and I succeeded. However, faith then took on another role in my life. It is one thing to trust God because of what you have heard or read that God has done for others. It is an entirely different story to trust God based on your own experience of His faithfulness. Not only did God do it for someone else and, therefore, could do it for me, God did it for me and, therefore, could do it again. Perhaps what makes the psalms so powerful is that often they speak of God's interaction and faithfulness to the writer. Psalm 23 does not read "The Lord is a shepherd, his people shall not want." It reads, "The Lord is MY shepherd, I shall not want." It is one thing to say that someone else found God faithful, but God wants to bring each of us to the place where, like David, we personally have found God faithful. David wrote, "I was young and now I am old, yet I have never seen the righteous forsaken or their children begging bread" (Ps. 37:25).

Listen to the testimonies of those who make up the "great cloud of witnesses" mentioned in the book of Hebrews (12:1). Listen to testimonies of those around you who have walked with God through the years. Listen to your own heart and mind as the Holy Spirit causes you to recall the miracles God has performed in your life and the "ways out of no-ways" He has made.

Section Three

All you Need is God

6

Why Should I Wait Any Longer?

How many people do you know who choose to provide for their own needs, identify their own spouses, register at the college they deem best and chart their own courses through life, because they simply believe they are better at making these decisions than God? I do not know one. Most people believe God knows best but do not wait on God because they find waiting too difficult a task. Some do not believe God will show up and others do not believe they can or should wait any longer.

A few years ago, I found myself in a strange place. I opened the refrigerator, freezer and cabinet and found they had something peculiar in common - they were all empty. I don't mean there was nothing in them I wanted to eat; there was nothing in them that would make a meal at all. In fact, while Elijah had baby food, my wife and Vaughn, Jr. had mashed potatoes for breakfast and I had grits. We were on our last meal. Although I could have called any of a hundred people or more to "help us out," some who had helped us in times past, this time I could not. It was not because of pride, it was because of maturity. After you have walked with God, talked with God and seen God show up at the eleventh hour, it becomes more difficult to simply go to others when you have a need before you go to God and wait for God's response.

I guess this is the part where I tell the awesome testimony of how we waited on God and because of our great faith, God showed up in miraculous fashion. Not so! Once the mailman left — you always wait for the mail carrier - we called for help. As reasonable as this sounds, I wondered if I had made the right choice – knowing to fail such a test would mean we would be destined to take it again. The next day I was unexpectedly given money from a family member. The day after, I received a check, not for me but for my ministry. The day after that, I received an unexpected reimbursement check from a business with which I was no longer affiliated.

What happened? Was the money the friend gave/loaned us supposed to hold us over until the other blessings arrived? Was God disappointed with us because we thought the mailman was the only possible vehicle by which the blessing could arrive that day? These are questions I cannot answer. Whether I passed the test and ended up in the center of God's will or failed the test and ended up in the center of God's mercy, the central point is God's faithfulness to us. The central point is God Showed UP! We can and should "hold unswervingly to the hope we profess, for he who promised is faithful" (Heb. 10:23). Yet, "if we are faithless, he will remain faithful ..." (2 Tim. 2:13a RV).

In the sixth chapter of 2 Kings, Benhadad, king of Syria, and his troops besieged Samaria causing a great famine to exist within the city. The famine was so extreme that the people ate the most horrendous of things. In fact, such things as a donkey's head and bird manure were counted as delicacies. No one would imagine that any amount or type of sin could make God's people deserving of such judgment. While the most faithful must have wondered where God was and when He would come to their rescue, one cry for justice caused Jehoram, the king of Israel to conclude that this perceived judgment from God would not end until the nation was totally destroyed. One day while out for a walk, a woman cried out for the king to help her. She had covenanted with a coworker to boil and eat their two children. After having surrendered her child on one day, the next day, the woman hid her child. King Jehoram proclaimed, "May God do so, and more also, to me, if the head of Elisha the son of Shaphat shall stand on him this day."

One can only imagine the horror this king must have felt. Although God alone could bring an end to the famine, the king was in charge. Although only God could provide for the nation, the king was the set man on the throne. There are very few, if any, worse feelings than one experiences when he or she is responsible for the provision and protection of others and find him or herself unable to provide and protect. The closest most of us come to this situation is when everything you have learned from childhood says, "You are the husband, you are the father, it is your obligation to work, provide for your family and protect them from all danger." However, you had no control over the downsizing. Despite your daily searches for work, you remain unemployed and the bills keep coming. Whether it applies to your situation or not, as you look in the empty refrigerator and check the empty cupboards one more time, the only scripture that comes to mind says, "If anyone does not take care of his own relatives, especially his immediate family, he has denied the faith and is worse than an unbeliever" (1 Tim. 5:8). It is during these times when we feel we cannot, we will not, just sit around and do nothing. How could we, why should we wait any longer for the Lord? This is where the king of Israel was and as his messenger reached Elisha the Prophet's home, he had only one question, "Behold, this evil is of Jehovah; why should I wait for Jehovah any longer" (2 Kings 6:33)?

When everything seems to be going wrong, when you have prayed, fasted, tithed and trusted but God has not shown up, there is a great temptation to go to "Plan B." Even so, there are important and very valid reasons to hold fast and wait for God.

The Right

We live in a postmodern age where many believe that right and wrong are merely subjective concepts. Profanity is neither right nor wrong, just a different way of expressing one's thoughts and feelings. Homosexuality is merely a different way of life based on one's preferences (what guides those preferences is not agreed upon). While pornography can be labeled "disgusting" on the local news, it is still very much legal in a country professing to be "one nation under God." Furthermore, other than child pornography, any laws against it are rarely, if ever, enforced. Perhaps teens and sex offer the best picture of where we are as a society in light of this chapter. Teens are encouraged to wait before having sex. They are not encouraged to wait until they are married. They are not even encouraged to wait until they are eighteen, have finished high school, or have known someone long enough to *think* they are in love. Teens are often encouraged to wait the same amount of time adults are willing to wait for what they want in life — until "they are ready." My wife insightfully stated, "It is amazing how society has set guidelines as to what age a person is ready to marry, smoke, drink alcohol, drive, etc. but allows children to determine when they are ready for sexual intercourse and the varied consequences of it." If one attempts to argue that drinking alcohol, smoking cigarettes and driving present certain dangers and costs to society when done prematurely or pre-maturity, he or she must then consider societal AIDS, teen pregnancy and abortion statistics. Even the argument for privacy falls apart at this point. A child drinking in private can create great havoc publicly. Teen sex presents no less of a threat to society. The health risks to the baby, such as low birth weight and malnutrition are often addressed via resources made available through tax dollars. As time progresses, statistics show that children born to teens, in addition to having health, social and emotional problems, are more likely to become incarcerated or to become teen parents themselves.

In addition to the increased risk for complications, such as premature labor during teen pregnancy, the more obvious statistics show that teen mothers are more likely to drop out of school and make less money than other mothers (http://www.women-shealth-channel.com/teenpregnancy/index.shtml). In light of the aforementioned, the negative results of refusing to label certain behavior as contextually right or wrong are undeniable. Perhaps in a different writing we will explore how we might address such hypocrisy. For now, it is enough for us to point out the hypocrisy of moral subjectivity and insist that there are rights and wrongs in the world and we ought to choose what is right, even if it means waiting beyond the period when we feel we are "ready."

Scripture teaches that despite the existence of life *and* death, right *and* wrong in the world, we are to choose that which pertains to life and that which is right. "This day I call heaven and earth as witnesses against you that I have set before you life and death, blessings and curses. Now choose life, so that you and your children may live" (Deut. 30:19).

Although the changes in our world seem to make it more difficult for people to determine what is right and what is wrong, I truly believe that, more often than not, honest and open study of scripture coupled with prayer will help us in this area. Note the words "honest" and "open." Sometimes it can be quite frightening to see how the scriptures have been taken out of context or used without regards to the character and nature of God in order to support warped agendas. Such demonic interpretations of scripture have been used to justify wars, oppress races and affirm various types of non-biblical relationships. An honest and open look means that we take down the "Do not Disturb" and "Keep Out" signs and allow the scriptures to do what God has intended them to do. "All Scripture is God-breathed and is useful for teaching, for reproof, for correction, and for training in righteousness, so that the man [or woman] of God may be complete and thoroughly equipped for every good work" (2Tim. 3:16-17 ISV).

The Apostle Paul wrote, "I have been crucified with Christ and I no longer live, but Christ lives in me. The life I live in the body, I live by faith in the Son of God, who loved me and gave himself for me" (Gal. 2:20). There was no question in Paul's heart about who was in charge of his life. In this sense Paul was like the Centurion who came to Jesus because his servant was about to die in Matthew Ch. 8 — Paul had authority but knew what it was like to be under authority. When we gave our lives to Christ, we enlisted in the Lord's army. On one hand, we do not have to "re-up" (or reenlist). On the other hand, we all need to "re-up" everyday. With each sunrise we must make the decision and commitment to live for Christ. Our daily affirmation should be that of Sylvana Bell & E.V. Banks who wrote, "I am on the battlefield for the Lord. I am on the battlefield for the Lord. And I promised Him that I would serve him till I die. I am on the battlefield for my Lord."

As it is in most of life, there is a penalty for not doing what is right. Jesus told a parable in Luke chapter 12 that addressed the fact that we will be held accountable for not doing good (what is right) — especially when we know to do it (see vv. 41-48). You will recall that in the book of Genesis we find the first offerings presented by Cain and Abel (Gen. 4). God was pleased with Abel's offering of the "first fruits" but had no respect for Cain's offering. Cain was livid! "Then the Lord said to Cain, 'Why are you angry? Why is your face downcast? If you do what is right, will you not be accepted? But if you do not do what is right, sin is crouching at your door; it desires to have you, but you must master it'" (Gen. 4:6-7). When we do what is right God is pleased. When we do not do what is right, the opportunity for sin to take a firm grasp of our hearts and rob us of our destinies is more real than we can imagine. Instead of Cain repenting, he allowed the spark of jealousy to burn out of control and he killed his brother. Sometimes the rationale for waiting on God is as simple as so many other things we are encouraged to do when growing up – it is simply the right thing to do.

The Response

Not only is it right to wait for God, we should wait for God because God will respond. In the passage I mentioned earlier from 2 Kings 6:33, the king's messenger relayed to Elisha, "This disaster is from the Lord. Why should I wait for the Lord any longer?" The very next words recorded were God's response through Elisha: "Hear the word of the Lord: thus says the Lord. This is what the Lord says: About this time tomorrow, a seah of flour will sell for a shekel and two seahs of barley for a shekel at the gate of Samaria."

While God's response will vary, God is faithful to respond. Jesus told a parable of a woman's experience with an unjust judge. It bears repeating.

Then Jesus told his disciples a parable to show them that they should always pray and not give up. He said: "In a certain town there was a judge who neither feared God nor cared about men. And there was a widow in that town who kept coming to him with the plea, 'Grant me justice against my adversary.' For some time he refused. But finally he said to himself, 'Even though I don't fear God or care about men, yet because this widow keeps bothering me, I will see that she gets justice, so that she won't eventually wear me out with her coming!' And the Lord said, "Listen to what the unjust judge says. And will not God bring about justice for his chosen ones, who cry out to him day and night? Will he keep putting them off? I tell you, he will see that they get justice, and quickly. However, when the Son of Man comes, will he find faith on the earth?" (Luke 18:1-8)

While many great sermons and writings have come from this passage, we must not, even for a minute, get away from why it was told in the first place... "Then Jesus told his disciples a parable to show them that they should always pray and not give up" (Luke 18:1). If the answers to our prayers were always to be imminent, if we were supposed to see the results by the time we brushed off our knees and fixed our faces, this parable would not have been necessary. I will say more about this parable in the chapter titled "The Waiting Room." For now, perhaps the greatest inspiration to be gained from it is found in that eighth verse. God will show up and those waiting on Him will be vindicated.

Another example can be seen in the fifth chapter of the Gospel of Mark.

When Jesus had again crossed over by boat to the other side of the lake, a large crowd gathered around him while he was by the lake. Then one of the synagogue rulers, named Jairus, came there. Seeing Jesus, he fell at his feet and pleaded earnestly with him, "My little daughter is dying. Please come and put your hands on her so that she will be healed and live." So Jesus went with him. A large

crowd followed and pressed around him...."
(Mark 5:21-24)

While this account of Jesus' encounter with Jairus begins all too typically, it soon turns tragic. People were often coming to Jesus and requesting the unusual and the perceivably impossible. Jairus' daughter had fallen deathly ill and if she was to recover, she needed divine intervention. Having pressed his way to see Jesus, Jairus stood on the brink of a miracle. Jesus consented to go with him and was on his way to heal his daughter. Then they were interrupted by a woman who had been suffering with chronic bleeding. Have you ever had an experience where you were depending on God to do something, were assured He would, and then everything came to a screeching halt? Jairus had not sent a servant to ask Jesus to come. He personally went to see Jesus. This was no time to be caught up with who he was or what title he held. He needed Jesus. Rather he thought his position might give him more immediate access to Jesus or that the mission was too important to put in anyone else's hands, he went himself. Jairus left the bedside of his dying daughter to seek out Jesus. What love! What faith! What determination! Jairus did not say, "Servant, you go. I want to be here just in case she passes." Jairus was too focused on doing everything possible to make sure she did not pass.

When it comes to life and death matters, frequently, we play it safe. We pray that someone will be healed but, just in case, we throw in, "But Lord, even if you don't..." Even when prophesying, many have a tendency to play it safe. I wonder how many times God is saying, "I want to be specific but you're prophesying generalities. I want to address details but you're giving them an overview." On too many occasions, we are afraid to throw caution to the wind and say what God says to say and do what God says to do. In the same way that Jairus had to let his daughter go in order for her to be healed, there are many situations and people that we must release in order to seek the One who is able to bring healing.

Having made such a faith-filled and radical decision to leave his daughter's side to find Jesus, I often wondered what went through Jairus' mind when Jesus stopped to see about the woman with the "issue of blood." Jairus' daughter was at Death's door and every second was precious. Perhaps in modern times it would have been like the paramedics on their way to the house of a heart-attack victim and stopping to tend to a person who had been stabbed in the leg. While the case may be made that Jairus' daughter was in far worse shape (after all, the woman had suffered with her condition for twelve years), for Jesus, this was not the issue. Jesus was not concerned about which situation was more severe or who got to Him first. If there was an issue that took priority with Jesus, it was one of faith. Faith stops Jesus every time. Jairus said, "Please come" (5:23). This woman said, "If I only touch..." (Mark 5:28).

As Jesus paused to interact with this desperate woman, hear the words of those from Jairus' house: "Your daughter is dead," the messenger said. "Why bother the teacher any more?" (Mark 5:35) Sound familiar? "Why bother the Teacher?" "Why should I wait for the Lord any longer?" Both questions seem to indicate there is no reason to expect a response from God. Have you ever been there? Have you ever been at a place where it seemed God had either no desire to respond or that it was too late for God to respond?

I am blessed to have a large number of friends. Some of those who are closest to my family are single or separated women who are waiting on God to do something miraculous in the area of marriage. The thing that has grieved me the most over the years has been God's apparent lack of response. I know some of these women wear beautiful masks but suffer in silence when it comes to their desire to marry (or have their marriages restored) and have children. At the same time, as biological clocks are ticking with a deafening sound in their heads, God has given some of them the grace to accept the possibility that they may not become mothers in the same way they once envisioned. The response some of them have received has not been the old playground nursery rhyme: "First comes love, then comes marriage then comes the mommy with the baby carriage." Instead, the response has been the gift of contentment within the role of teacher, aunt, godmother, etc. In the meantime, God's promise to respond to the marriage question stands sure. As they and many others wait, we too should wait for God. We wait not only because it is right, but also because at the proper time God will respond.

The scenario in Mark 5 continues not with Jesus responding to those who came from Jairus' house with the report of death but directly to Jairus – "Ignoring what they said, Jesus told the synagogue ruler, 'Don't be afraid; just believe'" (v.36). As we read on, Jesus did not merely respond with words. His words were followed by action.

> He did not let anyone follow him except Peter, James and John the brother of James. When they came to the home of the synagogue ruler, Jesus saw a commotion, with people crying and wailing loudly. He went in and said to them, "Why all this commotion and wailing? The child is not dead but asleep." But they laughed at him. After he put them all out, he took the child's father and mother and the disciples who were with him, and went in where the child was. He took her by the hand and said to her, "Talitha koum!" (which means, "Little girl, I say to you, get up!"). Immediately the girl stood up and walked around (she was twelve years old). At this they were completely astonished. He gave strict orders not to let anyone know about this, and told them to give her something to eat. (Mark 37-43)

In both Mark Chapter 5, and in Second Kings Chapter 7, we find the answer to King Jehoram's question, the same question asked by many in the most difficult situations—"Why wait?" Jairus' daughter was healed. About twenty-four hours after the prophet spoke with Jehoram, "a seah of flour was being sold for a shekel and two seahs of barley for a shekel at Samaria's gate" (7:1). Why wait? Because God will respond!

7

The Necessity of the Wait

Perhaps one of the most irritating things about worshipping a sovereign God is that God chooses to speak and act when, how and if He wants. As you very well know, there are times when God is silent. When God does respond to our requests the answer is most often "Yes," "No" or "Wait." As long as we have ears to hear what the Spirit of God is saying, we are delighted with God's "YES." Albeit disappointing, mature Christians are able to accept God's "NO" and go on with life. But what about when God says wait? W. A. I. T., for most, is among the worst of "four-letter" words and one of the most difficult of all of God's commands.

In John's gospel, chapter 11, Martha said, "Lord, if you had been here my brother would not have died." Martha thought that she had been waiting on Jesus to come and *do* something. But she was waiting on Jesus to come and *reveal* something. When God says something, it is already done in the spirit and only needs to be revealed or unveiled in the natural. Jesus had already said that Lazarus' sickness was not unto death. Therefore Jesus only needed to reveal to those in the natural what God had already done in the spirit realm. We should not imagine this was an isolated incident; God is still doing things in the spirit realm and then revealing those things to us in the natural realm. I do not believe that, while sitting in heaven, God sees a man walk into a coffee shop, and while the man is talking to the cashier, says, "Now there are two people who would make a nice couple." I believe that God has already identified the person He has called for each of us who are called to marry. We only need to have what has been planned in heaven to be manifested on earth.

While Lazarus lay at death's doorstep, Mary and Martha waited. Although Jesus' decision to make them wait appeared to be cruel and unusual punishment, the wait was necessary. Years ago, it was not unusual for a doctor to make a home visit. The more serious the ailment, the more likely a person was to receive a visit and the faster the doctor would come. In addition, the sisters did not merely call for Jesus to see about a neighbor, a colleague or someone Jesus met while passing through the area. They called for Jesus to come and see about someone Jesus "loved." In fact, John reiterates this just before he tells us that Jesus waited: "Now Jesus loved Martha and her sister and Lazarus. So when he heard that Lazarus was sick, he stayed where he was two more days, and then he said to his disciples, 'Let us go back to Judea'" (vv

5-7). Jesus' love for this family did not negate their need to wait. Actually, the way it is worded, it makes one question if it was partially the cause for the wait. Not only does the Lord "discipline" those He loves (Heb. 12:6), he also makes them wait.

When God told Habakkuk that the vision (from the Hebrew word "chazown"— a sight (mentally) i.e. a dream, a revelation) was for an appointed time, he was not referring to something uncreated that had yet to be manufactured. The vision was something that had already been created but would not arrive at where he was until the time designated by God. The thing that God had already created and shown to Habakkuk had a definite appointed time. Those who had not received the same revelation or seen the same vision would see it at that time.

Like a train, the vision had a scheduled stop at Habakkuk's place. It would tarry like a passenger train having to pick up or drop off passengers, but it would not linger as it pressed its way to its appointed destination. Habakkuk was instructed to wait for it.

Be encouraged! You are not waiting for God as much as waiting for the physical manifestation of what God has already caused to happen in the spirit. That manifestation has a time attached to it. Orson Wells once starred in a popular Paul Masson wine commercial whose slogan touted, "We will serve no wine until its time." This concept is great for wine commercials, but most of us in the real world want what we want when we want it despite the season. I recall one summer morning pulling up to a McDonald's drive through and requesting what I thought was an every day menu item. I was shocked and quite upset to learn that this particular McDonald's restaurant and several others did not sell hot chocolate during the summer months. For those of us who want Rita's water ice in December and hot chocolate in July, it is difficult to wait on a God who often withholds blessings until the appropriate season. Still, as the Apostle Paul wrote to the church at Galatia, "Let us not become weary in doing good, for at the proper time we will reap a harvest if we do not give up" (Gal. 6:9). A prerequisite to our reaping is that we not grow weary in doing well or doing what pleases God.

For Habakkuk the vision was for an appointed time. Paul assured the church at Galatia it was in due season (or at the proper time) that they would reap. Yet we want to win an Olympic gold medal before we finish the tryouts or even our training regiments.

According to Romans 12:15 we are to rejoice with those who rejoice and weep with those who weep. We are called to push envy, jealousy and covetousness aside and celebrate someone else's successes and blessings. Because we are family, because we are members of the body of Christ, we are expected to get excited when our brother or sister has a promise fulfilled. However, amid our rejoicing for others, there is often a haunting and seemingly unavoidable question that invades our thoughts and prayers: *When's my turn? When is my due season?* This word, "due," "idios" in Greek, can be translated "own." Strong's Concordance states that idios means "pertaining to self, own, one's own, private or separate - his, hers, ours, thine, yours, theirs or proper." The word "season" is from the word "kiros" and Strong's Concordance defines it as "an occasion or proper time." Therefore, the phrase "due season" means each of us has his or her own proper time or season that is specific to what God has in mind for our lives. Let me use my family as an example. My brother Andre, my sister Chaneta and I may each be waiting for God to pay off all of our bills and to bless us monetarily so we can be bigger blessings to our families, churches and those in need. However, according to the definition of "due season" we cannot expect that God will perform this in each of our lives at the same time. There is a Vaughn Foster season or time; there is an Andre Foster time; there is a Chaneta Redding time. There is also a time, or season, God has appointed for you.

Your time is not my time. The problem is we often spend far too much time at the docks observing someone else's ship coming in and we never checked the schedule to find out what time our ship is due. Although God may not always tell us when He will do something, like the sons of Issachar (1 Chron. 12:32), we need to understand the times so that when our season arrives, we know what we should do. Often we want someone else's season for marriage, children, healing, deliverance, or financial break-through, to be ours. However, we may not be prepared yet. Only God knows our individual preparedness and the season that ensures his blessing will be a blessing and not a curse.

Have you ever cracked open a hard-boiled egg that was not so hard-boiled inside? Perhaps the greatest reason for the delay, the necessity of the wait, is that we have not been boiled enough. We must stay in the water a little longer. Right now if we were removed from the situation, if the "shell" were to be taken off and we were exposed, there would be a mess.

This analogy is definitely suited for those waiting to launch out into full-time ministry. I have been there. Others were licensed, ordained, and sent out. I sat and I waited. Despite celebrating the fulfillment of others' seasons, I wanted to know, "When is my turn?" However, often it is in those final phases of waiting that we receive what we need to handle what awaits us when we are finally launched into our ministries. After a car is completed with all of the essential parts, it is painted and a special coating is applied over the paint. This coating prevents the paint from wearing out quickly when pelted by rain, snow, sleet, etc. Without this final phase, it would not be long before the vehicle would rust thus exposing the essential parts. Despite how it feels, even the latest phase of our waiting period is crucial to our development and preparation for our ministries, marriages, etc.

Each of us has an appointed time for the fulfillment of God's promises to us and it is necessary for us to wait for our own season. If you put a steak on the grill, you will not leave it on the same amount of time as you would a piece of chicken. One woman may carry her baby nine months, another eight and a half. Another woman may carry about nine months and two weeks. When the babies come out, they all seem to weigh about the same but they each have their own time. Most mothers know that it is not uncommon for the doctor to say, "You will deliver on August 8, give or take a few days." This is because each woman has her own time. God is saying, "Before I can bring to pass what you've been waiting for, you've got to enter into your time. You are still journeying and have not arrived there yet. It's not like I have to bring IT out, I have to bring you in - into your season."

It is amazing how we sit in the middle of winter wondering when the trees will bud. They will bud, but only in their time. Have you been asking, "When's my time?" If you have begun to grow frustrated and have said, "I want my time now," do not grow weary and do not faint. That word "weary" is the opposite of patience. In the words of the writer of the book of Hebrews, "So do not throw away your confidence; it will be richly rewarded. You need to persevere so that when you have done the will of God, you will receive what he has promised. For in just a very little while, He who is coming will come and will not delay" (Heb. 10:35-37).

I need patience; and I suspect you need patience. According to *Strong's Hebrew and Greek Dictionaries* (SHGD), this particular word for patience in Greek means "to be hopeful, to be cheerful, to have endurance or constancy, enduring, patience, continuance in waiting." What it means is that we do not walk around pacing the floor. We are hopeful. It is not as if we do not think it is going to happen.

When we have this kind of patience, we are just waiting for our season. It is like the example I used of the train. "Okay, I guess another five minutes and it will be here." We do not walk up and down the platform. The problem is that most of us think we missed our train because our spiritual clocks are broken. We do not know the will of God so we do not know where we are as it pertains to the will of God. When we are out of touch with God and therefore cannot do the will of God, it is kind of like standing around at the wrong train station. Things do not click on the job because we are on the wrong job. The relationship never gels because we are with the wrong person. The ministry never flourishes because the church simply wanted to fill the pulpit and the minister simply wanted a job.

Without question, we have need of patience. We have need of endurance. We need to be cheerfully hopeful while we are hanging in there so that we can do the will of God. We need this because there are only three places we can be: before the will, in the will or after the will of God. The reaping comes *after* we have done the will. Some of us are before the will of God; we have not even begun -like an egg sitting in the carton in the refrigerator. Some of us are in the will of God but we need to stay there for a season. It is as though we are in hot water, waiting for the very elements and circumstances that have the potential to destroy us, to make us into what we are called to be. It is on the other side of the boiling, after we have done the will of God that we receive the promise. God says, "You're asking, 'when's my turn?' Get up out of the carton. Until you get out of the carton and get into My will, don't even think about receiving the promise."

To those of us who are in the will, God is saying, "Hang in there! It's coming. I am going to do what I said I would do. Endure. Be patient." It is like being in second grade and wanting to graduate from college. You have to finish your current course. I have to finish my current race. We have to finish the course we are on before we get to the next one.

I really enjoy sports, especially when my son or one of my favorite teams is playing. Very rarely do you ever see the same kind of emotion at half time as you do at the end of a game. Can you imagine players running off the court cheering because they are up by thirty points after the first quarter or half and then sleeping for the rest of the game? Can you imagine after taking the lead for the first lap of a race, deciding on the second lap you will just walk? The Greek word translated "weary" in Galatians 6:9 means to lose heart, faint or relax. Sure, sometimes it is difficult to "Just Say No." It is much easier to sit than to stand, to relax than to run. Yet, if we do not start strolling, if you do not relax your values, if I do not relax my convictions, then, in each of our "due seasons," we will reap. If you are waiting for God to pay your bills, do not relax your convictions and go to the lottery line. If you are waiting for God to give you a spouse, do not grow weary and settle for a warm body or someone who simply does not love Jesus the way you do. It is when we lose heart during the wait that God says, "Okay, we have to do another lap."

As difficult as it may sometimes be to wait on God, the wait is necessary. It is after we have accomplished the will of God without losing heart or fainting, that in our own seasons, we will reap what God has promised.

Section Four

In the Waiting Room

8

The Waiting Room

The promises of God and their fulfillment existed within the heart of God before the foundations of the earth. Still, when God speaks a promise to us, it is not instantly fulfilled before our eyes. The apostle Paul wrote to the church at Rome, "But if we hope for what we do not yet have, we wait for it patiently" (Rom. 8:25). We are to hope for (better translated from Greek **"expect"**) the fulfillment of God's promises and patiently wait for them. Unfortunately, the waiting room can be filled with anxiety, apathy and allurement.

Many of us have gone through or are going through circumstances and situations we would rather not go through. Marriage problems, physical illnesses, financial struggles and/or character issues cause some to wrestle in silence. Others wrestle publicly, requesting the intercession of the body of Christ. Often the areas in which we struggle and in which we look for God to move seem innumerable. Despite our faith confession, or utter desperation, the provisions, the deliverance, the healing we need and expect from God seems to come much too slowly.

Perhaps the most frustrating place in life is where we find ourselves waiting, not simply for what we want, but for what God promised. This is a place where we read in the word or hear by the Spirit that God desires certain things for us. After reading 3 John 1:2, we believe that both John and God desire that we would prosper and be in health. One scarcely needs more than a Sunday school education to conclude that it is God's will that our families would be made whole, our children would be delivered, that our bills would be paid and that we learn to live within our means. There are certain areas in which we do not have to wonder what the will of God is — we know. Perhaps we have even heard a prophetic word about them - "Thus says the Lord, 'I'm going to resurrect the marriage'; 'I'm going to heal your body'; 'I'm going to fix your finances.'" You ask, "Lord, am I supposed to go through this all my life?" The answer comes, "No." From the time you get that "No," you enter the Waiting Room.

It is as though we have a loved one who is in the hospital and the doctors assure us that it is a delicate operation but they have complete confidence that the patient is going to pull through and that everything is going to be fine. Therefore, all we need to do is sit back and wait while they do what they have to do. While we have the assurance, almost the guar-antee, from the doctors that everything is going to be fine, we still pace the floor, bite our nails and pull out our hair because in the Waiting Room there can be anxiety.

In our individual, private waiting rooms, even after God says, "I'm going to perform it," there is often still anxiety. Although we do not have the experience, training, or credentials to assist the doctors in the procedure being performed, our anxiety compels us to do something. How many times have we heard it said, "Don't just stand there, do something?" Anxiety beckons us to act beyond our authority and despite our inability to change our situation. In Matthew's gospel, Jesus asks, "Who of you by worrying can add a single hour to his life" (Matt. 6:27)? The implied answer is "no one." Still, we often step out into unknown territory and try to alter our destinies, not through surrendering to God in our situation, but by playing god of our situation. Perhaps one of the clearest biblical examples of anxiety turned tragedy is in the life of King Saul. Saul's anxiety drove him to function outside of his calling and was largely responsible for his losing the kingdom.

Samuel stated he would meet with Saul within seven days. When the time had elapsed and Samuel had not arrived at Gilgal, Saul began to worry. As the people began to disperse, Saul decided to conduct the burnt offering and peace offerings in Samuel's place. As soon as he had finished offering the burnt offering, Samuel arrived. No excuse, no circumstance, no emergency could justify Saul's faithless response to his internal anxiety. If Saul thought the circumstances that "forced" him to disobey God's commandment would somehow justify his actions, he was sadly mistaken. Saul would be replaced by "a man after *God's* own heart," David. (1Sam. 13:8-14) Saul stands as an example to us that despite the promises of a future that is brighter than the sun, we must be aware of the anxiety that often accompanies our wait.

The problem with anxiety is not only that it sometimes pushes us into making faithless decisions. Anxiety is also what often immobilizes people, preventing them from seizing the promise. Many of us have personally known or have heard of someone who died of a curable disease because their fear of doctors, hospitals or surgery kept them from getting the help they needed. Then there was the relationship from ... well, wherever it was from it was not from God. Some have prayed for a husband or wife after God's own heart. However, the person they were with was clearly not the answer to their prayer. Still the anxiety of having to live the rest of life alone caused them to have a "bird in the hand" mentality. You know, "a bird in the hand is worth two in the bush." This mindset says, "I would rather settle for what I have than to risk it for better." This mindset can be anxiety based stating, "He may sell drugs but he's mine." "She may not love God like I do but she loves me." It says, "They may not be the distant promise fulfilled but they are here right now." Anxiety can both make us act when we should be still and it can cause us to remain in relationships, jobs, medical conditions and other situations that do not even resemble the promise of God.

In addition to anxiety, in the waiting room, there is also apathy. While few of us will admit it, we are, have been or will be at the place where we grow so weary in waiting for God that we cease to look for Him to fulfill the promise He made to us. You have been praying for a husband since you were eighteen-years-old. Now that you are forty-five you could not care less if God sends one or not. You have struggled with an illness or a spirit-crushing job for so long, you have resigned to be in that state for the rest of your life. Each prophetic word promising change is more of an annoyance than a blessing. Although you may smile, lift your hands and say, "Hallelujah," in your heart you say, "Yeah, yeah, I know - you are going to bring it to pass - whatever."

Even the spiritually mature among us have gotten to the place where we are not looking for another word from God. I recall a season where the last thing I wanted or could stand was another word from God. My feelings were simple, "God, why do I need another word when you have not fulfilled the last word? I am still waiting for you to bring the last promise to pass." I not only desired a word for others, I depended on God to give me one and was grateful when He did. Nevertheless, when promises God made to the church and to me were unfulfilled after five, six, seven years, I was not looking for another promise. We dare not talk about it among the "faithful" but sometimes while waiting for God we get tired, fed up, exhausted, and we just do not care the way we used to care. Jesus, at the end of a parable that was told for the purpose of our waiting room experiences asked, "… when the Son of Man comes, will he find faith on the earth" (Luke 18:8)? The fulfillment of the promise will happen. He will show up. However, will we grow apathetic in the wait? Certainly, there can be apathy in the waiting room.

Along with the anxiety and apathy one may experience while in the waiting room, it is critical for us to guard our hearts against the allurement that can also be found in the waiting room. Allurement is simply that which "attracts and draws." James wrote, "But each one is tempted when, by his own evil desire, he is dragged away and enticed" (James 1:14). Deleazo, the Greek word translated as "enticed" means "to entrap, beguile, or allure." The allurement found in the waiting room is not a natural element indigenous to waiting rooms. Allurement is imported specifically for the purposes of impeding our growth within and our progression through the waiting period.

Prior to Jesus' public ministry, he was led into the wilderness and there the devil sought to disqualify him for the ministry and mission before him (Matt. 4). Jesus hears a very similar challenge at the end of his earthly ministry as well. While hanging on the cross, shouts came from the crowds, the religious leaders and even one of the criminals hanging next to him to save himself. (Matt. 27:39-42 and Luke 23:39)

The allurement to exercise authority or power in order to relieve the discomfort of relying on God in times of need is more real than one can imagine - until the temptation begins. There is something in our human nature that says, "Save yourself!" This does not mean much when you are like Peter, terrified by the waves and sinking with nothing to hold on to but the divine hand that alone can save (Matt. 14:29-31). The real temptation or allurement comes when we have the ability to change our situation.

When I served as pastor of Grace Baptist Church, on my office walls hung photos I had taken from various meaningful places in my life. In addition, just above my computer desk hung my ordination certificate and diplomas. The diplomas did not just have the power to remind me of God's grace, mercy and provision. These symbols did not merely have the power to help me to recall the journey I had taken or to pinpoint my location on the road of my calling. These beautifully displayed documents had the power to allure me from my present place of ministry to a place where life would be presumably easier, more prosperous, less like foreign mission work. With all of my education and experience, certainly I had the ability to locate a ministry setting that required less and offered more. Certainly there was a place where there were more willing hands to help with the work. Certainly there was a place where there were more financial resources to fund the work and to enable me to provide for my family. Certainly, with these credentials, I qualified for the greener grass on the other side of the fence.

In Matthew 4, Satan tempts Jesus with three temptations. Each of the temptations offered Jesus the opportunity to change his current situation or mission. If Jesus changed the stone to bread, *He* could address his hunger. If he were to throw himself down from the temple not only would *He* prove who He was to Satan (who already knew), *He* would prove it to the people who would see the angels swoop down and catch Him before He "dashed His foot against a stone." Perhaps their seeing this would make his journey to the cross unnecessary. Satan's offer to trade all that Jesus came to rescue for a bit of worship placed Jesus in the position where He could determine by what means He would rescue humanity. However, while submitting to any of these temptations may have appeared a painless way of accomplishing the same thing, the end could never justify the means. In fact, such means could never render the end or results the Godhead desired and planned before the foundations of the world. Jesus had to stick to the script and fulfill the plan laid out by the Father.

As we ponder the various allurements in the waiting room, we must remember that they can never produce the results God has in mind. They look good, sound good and sometimes feel good, but they often do not represent God's plan for our current situation or the future we await.

9

Addressing the Anxiety

If it sounds as though what I am calling the waiting room is more like a minefield, it can be. The waiting room can be filled with temptations and distractions that not only delay the fulfillment of God's promises, they can cause us to shift so far out of the will of God that certain promises become null and void. Therefore, while we are in the waiting room, we must not simply wait; we must become engaged with those things that keep our hearts and minds focused on the things of God.

It seems inevitable that one will become anxious, apathetic and give in to the allurements found in the waiting room. While it may be inevitable that the phone will ring, you do have a say as to whether you answer it. Make no mistake about it, like annoying telemarketers or politicians during an election year, the devil has your number. He has my number too. What we need is spiritual Caller I.D. When we notice that the caller is not someone with whom we need to be engaged, we can simply not pick up. "Simply?" Well, often it is not so simple to ignore the enemy when he calls. In fact, even if we do not answer the phone we are too quick to check the message. It amounts to the same thing. Whether we listen to what the enemy has to say directly or indirectly, we often listen and it produces anxiety and apathy within us and becomes an allurement that draws or drags us to places we do not need to go.

The method to address anxiety is not as foreign to us as we might think. The Apostle Paul wrote, "Do not be anxious about anything, but in everything, by prayer and petition, with thanksgiving, present your requests to God" (Phil. 4:6). The scripture commands us "Do not be anxious," as if we have a choice in the matter. We do. The reason Paul did not write, "Try to avoid anxiety" or "Try not to let things worry you" is because he spelled out the formula that both shields us from anxiety and dispels any anxiety we may already have. The formula is prayer, petition and thanksgiving.

Prayer

The word translated as prayer does not mean, "To ask God." Why should it when "petition" means, "to ask?" This particular word for prayer (proseuche' in Greek), shows up no less than thirty-seven times in the New Testament. It can be understood to mean worship. However, the verses in which it is used suggest that it is a type of prayer that is intense, intimate communication with God. The focus of proseuche' is not whether a request is being made or not. Rather, it focuses on the fact that the person praying is in passionate dialogue with God at a level where he or she receives from God supernatural strength to do what must be done, endure what must be endured and overcome any obstacle that would hinder him or her from fulfilling destiny.

This type of prayer is required in order to cast out certain demons (Matt. 17:21, Mark 9:29). Because this type of prayer was to be the trademark of the temple, Jesus said "my house should be the house of proseuche'." (Matt.21:13, Mark 11:7) When Jesus says, "If you believe, you will receive whatever you ask for in prayer," (Matt. 21:22) he is speaking of proseuche. This type of prayer is characterized by on-going communication between a relational God and His people. To believe this God has already heard and answered the prayer is far less difficult under these circumstances.

In Luke 6 Jesus is in the midst of healing people with diverse afflictions. When he heals a man with a withered hand, the religious leaders are in an uproar and want Jesus dead. He spends the night in prayer and then summons the twelve and calls them apostles. It is unclear if it simply was customary for Jesus to pray through the night, if the contract on his life led him to pray, or if the need to make critical staff decisions was his motivation. However, it was clear that, having done so, Jesus was able to make the decisions he had to make and continue with his mission.

Certainly, this was not a "Now I lay me down to sleep …" prayer.

There are other examples but let me use just one more - perhaps the greatest. When Jesus knew his mission was nearing the end and the temptation to circumvent the cross was greatest, he prayed this type of prayer. If proseuche' were all about asking it would mean little in light of the fact that you may not get what *you* want. What we see in the words Jesus prayed that night is that he wanted out, "may this cup be taken from me." At the same time, while intimate communication with God expresses what we want, it always listens to and receives what God wants - "Yet not as I will, but as you will" (Matt. 26:39).

Songwriter Cleavant Derricks wrote. "Let us have a little talk with Jesus, let us tell him all about our problems, he will hear our faintest cry and he will answer by and by." While proseuche' may not necessarily mean a "little" talk with Jesus it does mean an intimate dialogue where we share what is on our minds and in our hearts. It does mean that we listen for God's response as well as look for it. It does mean when we have concluded our time together we are equipped for the next phase of our journey and mission. It is during such a talk, through such dialogue, that we ought to cast all of our anxiety on God knowing that he cares for us (1Pet. 5:7).

Petition

In addition to our communication with God through prayer, Paul instructs the believers to petition God. The old Negro "call and response" song proclaims, "Jesus on the mainline - tell Him what you want, Jesus on the mainline - tell Him what you want, Jesus on the mainline tell Him what you want, call Him up and tell Him what you want." What sense would it make if my eleven-year-old sat in his room crying and worrying because he had not eaten instead of asking for food? Can you imagine him sitting there saying to himself, "Now it looks like the sun is setting and the last time I checked there was not much food in the refrigerator. I am really getting worried that I may not eat tonight." Thank God, my son never has to worry about whether he will eat, drink or have clothes to wear. He only needs to ask. He may not always have what he wants but he will always have what he needs. When it seems as though he does not have anything to wear it may be in the wash. His next meal may not be on the table at the exact moment he wants to eat but it is definitely "in the works." We do not need to worry; we need to petition.

While petitioning is asking, and we ought to ask for what we want, James gives us specific parameters. We must also "... believe and not doubt, because he who doubts is like a wave of the sea, blown and tossed by the wind" (James 1:6). We also must make sure our motives are right. He warns the readers, "You ask and do not receive, because you ask with wrong motives, so that you may spend it on your pleasures" (James 4:3 NAS). It is the asking God that demonstrates our dependence on and trust in God. It is asking with proper motives that demonstrates our spiritual maturity and our being in tune with the very heart of God.

In Psalm 37 David says, "Delight yourself in the Lord, and he will give you the desires of your heart." This psalm, while not specifically addressing the act of petitioning God, does say how one gets what he or she wants from God. Instead of pacing, pouting or pleading, one should focus on pleasing - pleasing God. The Hebrew word translated here as "delight" also means soft or pliable. It is as we delight ourselves in the Lord or are pliable, soft and moldable to His will, that God gives us not the lusts of our flesh, or whims of our minds, but the desires of our hearts. When we know the types of prayers God longs to hear and answer, it is easier for us to cast fear aside and petition God for what is on our hearts - and His.

Thanksgiving

The last ingredient to this anxiety-dispelling recipe is thanksgiving. Some have read this verse and concluded that it means that we should thank God for what we have asked for as though we have already received it. Others insist that it means as we petition God for what we need or desire, we ought to simultaneously thank God for past prayers that have already been answered, ways already made and provisions already supplied.

There are two crucial things to remember when considering these differing interpretations. First, much like this book, in this passage Paul is not primarily concerned about the reader getting what she or he wants from God. Paul's primary concern, at least in this passage, is helping the reader to have peace in the very situations that often cause us great stress and anxiety. Secondly, Paul is not writing about faith. When Jesus said, "That is why I tell you, whatever you ask for in prayer, believe that you have received it and it will be yours" (Mark 11:24 ISV), He spoke of the faith one should have while praying to receive something from God. Albeit, in this particular situation when Paul speaks of thanksgiving he is not talking about the recipe for getting anything we want or need from God, other than the peace of God. Thanksgiving is not a tool to get more from God.

John wrote, "And this is the confidence that we have in him: if we ask for anything according to his will, he listens to us. And if we know that he listens to our requests, we can be sure that we have what we ask him for" (1 John 5:14-15 ISV). It is very appropriate to thank God for hearing us. You might recall, Jesus thanked the Father for hearing Him before he raised Lazarus from the grave: "Father, I thank you that you have heard me. I knew that you always hear me, but I said this for the benefit of the people standing here, that they may believe that you sent me" (John 11:41b - 42).

By faith, one might even thank God for receiving it before it actually arrives on the table, at the bank account, or in the home. Yet, as one studies the prayers found in the Bible, especially the prayers of petition found in the Hebrew Scriptures, it is apparent that most of them include thanks for something God had already done. With this in mind, I believe Paul is encouraging the readers to enter into intimate dialogue with God and petition God while having an attitude of gratitude for what God already did at the same time.

I would love to be able to say that the first time I learned of the word "ingrate" it was while reading a novel, watching television or even hearing a sermon. The truth is the first time I heard the word it was being applied to my brother, sister or me - perhaps all three of us. Few things are worse than asking for something when we have not articulated or demonstrated an appreciation for what we have already been given. Even worse, we pray and pray and pray for a spouse. God blesses. Not only do we fail to thank God for such an amazing gift, we fail to show any appreciation for the gift. Like the once new car with the french fries and cookie crumbs on the floor, tears in the seats and months of dirt caked on it, we sometimes treat our spouses like something we picked up while at the dump rather than something sent from heaven.

Perhaps the most important part of gratitude is that it connects the recipient of the gift to the giver through the gift. The gratitude we express to God through thanksgiving not only blesses the heart of God, it blesses us. Johnson Oatman, Jr. wrote, "When upon life's billows you are tempest tossed, when you are discouraged, thinking all is lost, count your many blessings, name them one by one, and it will surprise you what the Lord hath done." Thanksgiving is more than our saying, "Lord I got it! Thanks for sending it!" Thanksgiving is our saying, "Lord I got it! You love me! I can trust you! You will take care of me!" In this, we lay hold of the very peace of God! When we look back on what God has done we are reminded of who God is. When we consider who God is and what God has done we are motivated to ask, "Is there anything too difficult for God?" The answer to that question can give us peace amid any storm - "No! There is nothing too difficult for God!" We will look at the necessity of thanksgiving again in chapter sixteen: *Just wanted to say thanks!*

Remember, the title of this chapter is "Addressing the Anxiety." Most people, most normal people reading this book want the pain to stop, the bills to be paid, the wait to be over. However, again, Paul's point here was not so much to teach the Philippians how to get what they wanted from God but how not to be anxious while in the waiting rooms of their lives. So often, we want deliverance and not development. The problem is this: whenever we go through something and are delivered *from* or *out of* it without being developed *by* the experience, we have suffered in vain. Peter put it this way:

> In this you greatly rejoice, though now for a little while you may have had to suffer grief in all kinds of trials. These have come so that your faith — of greater worth than gold, which perishes even though refined by fire — may be proved genuine and may result in praise, glory and honor when Jesus Christ is revealed. (1 Pet. 1:6-7)

James encourages the saints that were dispersed throughout Asia, Greece, Egypt, Italy and perhaps other areas,

> Consider it pure joy, my brothers, when you are involved in various trials, because you know that the testing of your faith produces endurance. But you must let endurance have its full effect, so that you may be mature and complete, lacking nothing. (James (1:2-4 ISV)

This really is not a new concept. What is new, but getting old fast is the concept of not suffering, not waiting, and not allowing "endurance to have its full effect." Paul wrote,

> ... but we also rejoice in our sufferings, because we know that suffering produces perseverance; perseverance, character; and character, hope. Hope does not disappoint us, because God has poured out his love into our hearts by the Holy Spirit, whom he has given us. (Rom. 5:3-5)

If not a quick fix to our problems, if not an easy way out of our dilemmas, what do we get? Peace! Paul writes that when anxiety is addressed with intimate dialogue with God, petitioning God and thanking God, we receive the peace of God. This amazing peace does not merely soothe our nerves but, according to the Greek translation of this passage, it guards our hearts (thoughts or feelings) and minds (perception, intellect, or disposition) through Christ Jesus. How awesome is that?

10

How Shall I Wait?

Worship: The Distraction of God's Presence

Key to our sustenance in the waiting room is worship. When we consider worship, we often view it as that which we offer God because of the awesome, wonderful, amazing God He is. This motivation is appropriate. We ought to worship God! My grandmother's generation often said, "If He doesn't do another thing for me, He's still worthy!" Our worship of God must be based on who God is and not what God does. "When we think of the goodness of Jesus and all He's done for us," we praise. However, worship expresses our knowledge of and acknowledgment of who God is. I vividly recall a service where I looked out and saw many of the parishioners sitting during praise and worship. It grieved me. The Spirit of God was moving in the service and some people were praising and worshipping. Still many just sat. One brother who had come in a wheelchair stood up on both feet. I was horrified! This brother had literally been run over by a truck but despite the pain and discomfort he experienced, he was determined to worship God. Others, who had been blessed, kept, provided for, etc. all week, sat on God. It was hard, so very hard not to just leave the service. However, the actions or inactions of some in the congregation on that day were perhaps more appropriate than I had understood at that time. When you know who God is, you are able to worship. When you know what God has done, you are able to praise. When you are not sure of either, the best you can do is follow instructions - "Put your hands together. Turn to your neighbor. Jump up and spin around. Lift your hands and say, 'Hallelujah'!" Jesus told the Samaritan woman who came to the well, "... a time is coming and has now come when the true worshipers will worship the Father in spirit and truth, for they are the kind of worshipers the Father seeks. God is spirit, and his worshipers must worship in spirit and in truth" (John 4:23-24).

We worship God because God is worthy of our worship. Still, one important benefit of worship is its ability to distract. More accurately, worship brings the One who is seeking worshippers into our presence and He distracts us by His presence. While distractions, by nature, are often negative, remember it was the burning bush that was not consumed that distracted Moses from his shepherding responsibilities (Exod. 3). Also, it was an angel of the Lord that distracted Zachariah while he was performing his priestly duties and told him of Elizabeth's impending pregnancy (Luke 1). Often, the presence of God comes to distract us from our daydreaming, our responsibilities and even our ministering in order to have us focus on that which is of even greater importance for that moment or season.

As one reads about the specifications of the temple in Jerusalem and the Ark of the Covenant, "Wow!" comes to mind. However, during the dedication of the temple, God showed up and the scriptures tell us "When the priests withdrew from the Holy Place, the cloud filled the temple of the Lord. And the priests could not perform their service because of the cloud, for the glory of the Lord filled his temple" (1 Kings 8:10-11). If the people wanted to focus on the temple, the Ark of the Covenant or even the priests, they could not because of the distraction of God's presence.

Can you imagine, after several years of fund raising and keeping the vision before the people; after spending months walking the land and millions of dollars purchasing it and building on it; after inviting family, friends, the community and the press, on opening day God shows up and distracts us from everything but His presence! There are two things that put me in awe of the Cathedral International in Perth Amboy, NJ. The first is the amount of time and preparation that goes into the Sunday morning service before the service ever begins. The second is how little time one has to appreciate all of the preparation because God's presence has a way of commanding one's complete attention from the time the service begins until it ends. Certainly we can choose to allow the singer's voice, the beautiful bulletins or the fine décor to arrest our attention. However, if we resist, at the Cathedral and at our own places of worship, we can be distracted by the presence of God. In the same way—if we will allow Him—God can and will distract us from many of the discomforts of the wait.

In the waiting room we must focus on who God is and our love for Him. People who are really in love sometimes do not eat, cannot sleep and, if not careful, can walk into walls or drive through red lights. Someone in love can become so distracted by the person who is the object of his or her affection that nothing else seems to matter. What a wonderful place to be while in the waiting room.

I don't mean that every time you worship you need to go into the sanctuary, kneel down, lift your hands, and worship. Albeit it is great when you are able to enter the sanctuary, kneel, etc., sometimes you have to worship right where you are.

So often, tragedy strikes when we are waiting on God to do something. But we have to get to the place where we say, "Lord, I'm going to worship You, anyhow!" Job said, "All the days of my appointed time will I wait, till my change comes" (Job 14:14 KJV). We must get to a point where cursing God and dying, as recommended by Job's wife (2:9), is not an option because we are too consumed by God's presence through worship. It is time for us to stop walking and worrying and start walking and worshipping. There is a real distinction between walking with your head bowed down and walking with your hands lifted up.

Work the Work

In addition to worshiping, we should work while in the waiting room. God has not called us to be busy for busyness' sake. If we are not careful, our doing will hinder our being. Still, Jesus said, "As long as it is day, we must do the work of him who sent me. Night is coming, when no one can work" (John 9:4). Though our first priority in the waiting room is worship, the truth is, it is hard to do meaningful work apart from worshiping. Have you ever been waiting for a call from the doctor's office, the bank or a relative and you had to go to work? While you were on the job trying to work, your mind was most likely back in the waiting room. You are waiting for the phone call, you are waiting for the healing, you are waiting for the deliverance, you are waiting for the way out, and all the while, it is difficult to focus on the work. Therefore, the best thing to do is to worship until you get your focus right and then get to work.

Work can be a wonderful distraction in the waiting room. I can still recall the months and weeks before our wedding some seventeen years ago. When I graduated from Lincoln University in May 1991, I had no idea that I would be the groom in a wedding to take place only three months later. As Lisa and I walked and talked about our relationship and engagement, we both sensed the wedding was destined to occur sooner than it was originally scheduled. We planned to marry in one to three years. However, heaven had another date on its calendar. Once we heard from God and received confirmation from those that mattered in such decision-making, we rescheduled for August. Albeit it was only three months away, the wedding date seemed much further. Well, that is until we started working. It was to be a small wedding so putting it together should have been a breeze. It wasn't! In fact, we were micromanaging every aspect of the wedding until the day after. As far as the wait was concerned, as we engaged in all of the preparation responsibilities and work, the months felt like days.

While waiting for God to do what He said He would do, we must make up our minds to worship and work. Hebrews 10:36 reads, "You need to persevere so that when you have done the will of God, you will receive what he has promised." Receiving the promise comes after we "do" or "work" the will of God. Seasons of silence are not times to sit around complacent. The truth is many of us think that "Wait on the Lord" means "Put your feet up, grab a bag of chips and a drink, and sit around until God shows up." At the same time, I do not believe God's definition of "wait" is to simply be busy doing things. So where is the balance? If we are not supposed to sit around with our feet up and we are not supposed to run around like a modern-day Martha – "worrying about all the things she had to do" (Luke 10:40 ISV), what are we supposed to do?

Have you ever really observed a waiter at a restaurant? A good waiter is expected to be both busy and still at the same time. The waiter I truly enjoy tipping is the one who takes my order, gets my food, refills my glass and shows up with the check when I am ready to go – all without hovering. I believe what makes a great waiter is that despite whatever should be done, needs to be done or could be done, a great waiter appears to have nothing to do until I ask for something. At that moment, he is in position, ready and willing to do what I need him to do. I believe I gave one of the largest tips I have ever given to a waitress who simply looked in my direction when I was ready to go. Over the years I had grown so annoyed with waiters and waitresses who never seemed to wait around long enough to see what I needed and almost always vanished when I was ready to go. So, when this one waitress saw me, amid her many responsibilities, I felt special and tipped her well. I truly believe the balance between waiting on God and working on the assignments given by God is much like this example. Although we have much to do, we should work with an ear listening for God's voice and an eye looking for His subtle gesture beckoning us to attend to whatever matter He presents. Like a waiter, while we are in the waiting room, or any other room, we should stand as though we have nothing to do except what God calls us to do. Certainly, we have to pour water for the people at Table 3 or take an order for the couple at Table 9. Still, our eyes should always be on God so that whatever He needs us to do, whenever He needs us to do it, we are ready, willing and able.

A few things to consider ... When you are in the waiting room and a loved one is having a procedure done, what are you supposed to be doing? Who else is in that waiting room with you? You might have some work to do. There may be someone in the waiting room with you who does not know Christ, who cannot handle the fear and uncertainty of their situation or the pressure of the wait. Sometimes the work we are to do while in the waiting room involves praying for others who are waiting for a spouse. Sometimes our work is to encourage someone else who also lost his or her job or has a loved one on drugs. The waiting room is where we share with others who may also be in trouble the very comfort we have received from God. The apostle Paul explained it this way, "Praise be to the God and Father of our Lord Jesus Christ, the Father of compassion and the God of all comfort, who comforts us in all our troubles, so that we can comfort those in any trouble with the comfort we ourselves have received from God" (2 Cor. 1:3&4). Our primary work in the waiting room is to comfort, strengthen and give biblical instruction to those who are in any trouble.

Despite our being confined to a place and a season of waiting, God still expects us to be at work until that season is completed. For some, waiting feels like a prison sentence. Well, neither you nor I have the option of just sitting in our cells. Certainly, Israel viewed their season of waiting in this manner when they were in captivity in Babylon and longed to return to their homeland. How natural it must have been to just sit by the rivers of Babylon, weep and reminisce of their beloved Zion (Ps. 137). Yet, God had destined them to more. Through Jeremiah God instructed them ...

Build houses and settle down; plant gardens and eat what they produce. Marry and have sons and daughters; find wives for your sons and give your daughters in marriage, so that they too may have sons and daughters. Increase in number there; do not decrease. Also, seek the peace and prosperity of the city to which I have carried you into exile. Pray to the Lord for it, because if it prospers, you too will prosper. (Jer. 29:5-7)

In a parable that both speaks to stewardship and waiting, Jesus said,

Who then is the faithful and wise servant, whom the master has put in charge of the servants in his household to give them their food at the proper time? It will be good for that servant whose master finds him doing so when he returns. I tell you the truth, he will put him in charge of all his possessions. (Matt. 24:45-47)

While we are in the waiting room, we have to work. In Ecclesiastes 9:10 it says, "Whatever your hand finds to do, do it with all your might, for in the grave, where you are going, there is neither working nor planning nor knowledge nor wisdom." Basically, you've got to do it now because once you're dead, it ain't gonna get done. Work the work now. Do what God has called you to do now. God has made you some promises; the waiting room is not the Promised Land and it cannot offer the wonderful things God has in mind for you. Still, you must not sit around mourning your situation. It is time to get to work - right where you are! While you are waiting on God and waiting for God, begin to worship and keep working!

Stay in the Will

Lastly, it is imperative that we stay in the will of God. While you are waiting, be in the will of God. If you are waiting for God to send you a financial blessing, what sense does it make to gamble away what you already have? If you are waiting for God to send you a spouse, what sense does it make to be sleeping around? If you are waiting for God to deliver your son from drugs, what sense does it make to give him money you know he will spend on drugs? Stay in the will of God doing what He would have you to do and being where He calls you to be. Where does God want you to wait? Sometimes I'll tell my son, Elijah, "Stand right there. I'll get your sandwich and your juice. Stay right there." More often than not, he'll move. We are no different. Whether we are being driven by our anxiety, our impatience, or curiosity, staying put is not always easy. No matter how uncomfortable the waiting room, few things could be worse than moving when God's will is for us to be still. In Acts 27, while being carried by ship to stand before Caesar, a storm arose and Paul, his companions and captors were in danger of going down. "In an attempt to escape from the ship, the sailors let the lifeboat down into the sea, pretending they were going to lower some anchors from the bow. Then Paul said to the centurion and the soldiers, unless these men stay with the ship, you cannot be saved" (Acts 27:30-31). We are sometimes called to stay on jobs or in situations longer than we would prefer. If we sense it is God's will, we would be better served to stay. Unless we do, we cannot be saved.

It goes back to Jesus' question, "when the Son of Man comes, will He find faith on the earth" or will He find us doing something else? Will we be distracted by the things of the world? I grieve when I think about how many times God opens a door for us and we are no longer prepared to go through it. It's like the little child in his or her Easter whites all ready for the Sunday School pageant. However, when it is time to go, you turn around and the child's clothes are all dirty. You cannot leave. You have to change his pants or you have to put her in a new dress. While the child was waiting, something allured him. "Ooh, what's that?" While you are in the waiting room, worship God, do the work you have been called to do and make sure you stay in God's will so the process He wants you to go through is not prolonged. Although God is patient, one cannot expect God to keep his loved ones waiting while we chase every distraction the enemy sends our way. If God calls a pastor to a church but the church ignores

Him, choosing to chase preachers with more style but little substance instead, eventually God will not simply "open a window" to replace the closed door for that preacher. He will open another door or knock down a wall to a much better place.

If you are in the waiting room, you are not being overlooked, in spite of what you have been thinking or feeling. When you are worshipping, He sees you. When you are working, He sees you. When you are in the will of God, He sees you. In fact, these are the times when you can be seen the best. Usually that person who is sleeping in the lounge is overlooked but the one who is working diligently is always in the manager's eyesight. God is aware of your state even when it seems He does not see you when you want or expect to be seen. In God's own time, He has a way of letting us know that we are not forgotten. I am reminded of Esther and Mordecai. Mordecai saved the king's life and he may, I don't know, have been waiting for a "Thank you." He would have waited and waited for that "Thank you" because it did not come until he really needed it (Esther 2:21-23 &6:1-11). Do you remember the cupbearer Joseph met while he was wrongly imprisoned? Joseph interpreted the cupbearer's dream, asking the cupbearer to plead Joseph's case before Pharaoh. Though he agreed to do it, once the cupbearer returned to his position, he forgot about Joseph! (Gen. 41) However, in God's season, when it mattered most, he recalled Joseph. The result of Joseph's God-given ability to interpret dreams and God's ability to bring him to the remembrance of the cupbearer at the perfect time was that the lineage of Abraham, Isaac and Jacob was saved and many others benefited from Egypt's stable commerce.

Some of us have been waiting for God to do something and God says, "I'm going to do that thing just when you need it the most." You might be waiting for the Social Security Administration to resolve your case. It will happen just when you need it the most. As William Poole wrote in 1907, "Just when I need Him most, Jesus is here to comfort and to cheer. Just when I need Him most!" Just when you look in the refrigerator and all you have left of a loaf of bread are the end pieces, He steps in, opens a door and makes a way – just when you need Him most. People tend to be resilient when facing trouble. How many times have you witnessed a marriage hanging on by a thread for years? How many times have you seen a family torn apart by drug addiction enable the addicted person for years? As much as it hurts, as hard as it is to face, sometimes it is only when the situation can be truly called "rock bottom" that we have no choice but to trust God. It is then, just when we need Him most, that Jesus is there — Just when we need Him most!

Let me say something else about Mary, Martha and Lazarus. When Lazarus got sick and they called for Jesus to come, it's as though Jesus looked at His watch and said, "What time is it? Oh, I've got plenty of time." Yet, when Jesus showed up, Lazarus was dead and had been dead for days. His sisters said, "Lord, if only you had been here, my brother would not have died" (John 11:21 & 11:32). But that's not really when they needed Him to be there. Jesus said, "This sickness is not unto death but so that God will get the glory" (John 11:4). This sickness was not to demonstrate Jesus' ability to heal. They had already seen that. What they needed to see and understand was that beyond being a healer, Jesus was, is and always will be the resurrection and the life. Therefore, with the words, "Lazarus, come forth!" the scripture says that "he that was dead got up." I can imagine that those who beheld this amazing event, especially those who removed the death shroud from Lazarus' body, told their families and friends for miles and for generations. This miracle was not just for Mary, Martha or Lazarus but so everybody there on that day and many others for ages to come would know who Jesus was.

You may have been in the waiting room longer than you anticipated. However, when God brings you out, it will not be just for your children to see it. It will not be just for your spouse to see it. It will not be just for your neighbors to see it. It will be for everyone around to see what a mighty God we serve! It was not enough just for the children of Israel to know God was a deliverer. After God destroyed the Egyptians, word of His greatness spread throughout the entire region. As the Egyptians pursued the people of God, God instructed Moses,

> Raise your staff and stretch out your hand over the sea to divide the water so that the Israelites can go through the sea on dry ground. I will harden the hearts of the Egyptians so

that they will go in after them. And I will gain glory through Pharaoh and all his army, through his chariots and his horsemen. The Egyptians will know that I am the Lord when I gain glory through Pharaoh, his chariots and his horsemen. (Exod. 14:16-18)

Not only did the Egyptians learn of God's faithfulness to His people, before long, every one would. When Joshua sent two spies to Jericho, Rahab told them,

"I know that the Lord has given this land to you and that a great fear of you has fallen on us, so that all who live in this country are melting in fear because of you. We have heard how the Lord dried up the water of the Red Sea for you when you came out of Egypt, and what you did to Sihon and Og, the two kings of the Amorites east of the Jordan, whom you completely destroyed. When we heard of it, our hearts melted and everyone's courage failed because of you, for the Lord your God is God in heaven above and on the earth below. (Josh. 2:9-11)

During our seasons of waiting, God is not trying to just do something for you and for me but He is trying to do something for everyone around us to see. God is glorified through our waiting room experiences and as He brings us out, His awesome works

will be known far and wide if we will worship, work
and stay in His will.

11

Behind Closed Doors

In addition to the work God performs in us while we are in the waiting room, more times than we may ever know, we are not the only cause for the wait. Let me explain it this way. When I was in seminary, for the first two years I had an amazing job. I served as youth pastor of a wonderful church under an amazing man of God. From the time I accepted Christ, I knew God was preparing me for ministry. My time at Mount Olive Baptist Church serving under and along side the Rev. Gregory Jackson was a great time of training. Without question, I am a better minister, husband and father because of some of the things I learned from him and the ministry I was able to offer while in Hackensack, NJ. However, I never considered remaining at Mt. Olive for the entire time I was in seminary. During a conversation with my pastor, Bishop Donald Hilliard, he indicated that he wanted me to come home for my final year of seminary so he could make sure I would be prepared for the pastorate. I did not view this as a parent calling his child in from the park just when he was having fun. I saw this as a concerned parent wanting quality time to evaluate his son's readiness for the very serious and sometimes overwhelming work of ministry.

When I left Hackensack and returned home my future was clear. I would serve at the Cathedral in some capacity then pastor a "well to do" church who would pay to move my family's things from Madison, NJ to the parsonage. I would enjoy fruitful ministry and be compensated well enough to pay off my student loans. None of these things came to pass when or how I expected. When I graduated from Drew University instead of entering a loving ministerial setting, I entered the waiting room. While in the waiting room I learned how to wait, worship and work in new ways. Every time I was given the opportunity to minister at Harvest Ministry, where my father-in-law is the founder and senior pastor, or at a vacant church (a church without a pastor), I could see God working in me and through me. However, there was much going on behind closed doors. There were times I felt, "Surely God can trust me with a congregation by now." Perhaps God could, perhaps He could not. What I later discovered was that while I was in the waiting room, Grace Baptist Church in Trenton, NJ and some of the members who joined soon after I arrived were in the operating room. There were wounds that needed to be healed, leaders that needed to leave and new members who needed to cast their gaze away from wherever they were so that God could draw them into Grace. Together, that small congregation and I survived some struggles that would have crushed many pastors and congregations. We were able to touch lives and bless the city in ways that could never have happened if I arrived when I thought I was ready to pastor.

Ministry is only one example. How many men are waiting for women still in the operating room? How many women are waiting for men still in the operating room? The truth is some who were less patient are checking the mail every day wondering when the recall notice will come: "Dear Sir or Madam, I regret to inform you that there has been a recall on your spouse. It appears that your spouse was put into operation prematurely. There is still very important work that needs to be done on him/her before he/she will be road-worthy. Please return your spouse to the place (and time if possible) where you obtained him/her so needed work may be performed. We do sincerely apologize for any inconvenience this may have caused you." No one likes to place or accept blame but it is often our own impatience that causes these kinds of problems. We do not want to submit to marriage counseling so we go to the Justice of the Peace. We do not want to delay physical gratification (as if that is all marriage is about) so we whip out the scripture that states, "It is better to marry than to burn" and use it to rebuke anyone who encourages us to extend the engagement or delay the wedding. What happens is the equivalent of wheeling a patient undergoing heart surgery out of the operating room before the defect is repaired because we are tired of walking around the waiting room. It is like snatching a patient out from behind closed doors prior to his or her brain surgery being complete because God promised us a woman or a man and we are unwilling to wait for the needed work to be performed.

So often, if the waiting room is what it is supposed to be, by the time the operation is done, we are prepared to see and receive. Could you imagine if in the middle of the operation, the doctors rolled your loved one out, bleeding all over the place? "Well we knew you really wanted to see him so here he is!" Can you imagine? Could you imagine being about to have a baby and the doctor says to the people in the waiting room, "I know everyone is getting worried so everyone come on in." Then he brings the whole family in! God is saying that "I am trying to do something but some things you cannot see right now. I have to do them behind closed doors with you in the waiting room. I need a sterile environment." Sometimes God has to shut out everything and everyone except those who have been handpicked and authorized to enter into the Holy of Holies. The account of Jairus' dying daughter is a good example (Mark Chapter 5). How many times in scripture were people put out so Jesus could do what He needed to do? People say, "But we love them, too." So often, God only allows the closest of the close to come in where the operation takes place. Everybody else has to stay in the waiting room.

Sometimes you cannot see what the Lord is up to so keep working. While you are working, and worshipping and God is doing His work, you're being prepared for what's on the other side. Just because we are not able to see what goes on behind closed doors, does not mean God is not at work. Applying what has already been written in the previous chapters will help us to have peace in the waiting room while God does what He needs to do behind closed doors. There is a man who needs surgery on his hands so he can get off the sofa and do some work. There is a congregation that needs heart surgery so it can stop beating down its pastor. There is a pastor who needs eye surgery so he can see the congregation as Christ's bride and the service as a time of worship and not a psychotherapy session where he goes to work out his childhood and life-long issues. Unlike surgeons in the medical profession who specialize in a particular area of expertise, God is multi-disciplinary. The types and numbers of surgeries He performs on individuals and institutions behind closed doors are too vast to list. Yet, we can rest assured that even behind closed doors "... He works all things together for the good of those who love God, who are called according to His purpose" (Rom. 8:28 ISV).

12

The Cloning of
God's Promise

No matter what we ask from God, no matter what we expect from God, what God is committed to is what He has promised. The Bible is laced with scriptures that tell us how important God's word is to Him. In Psalms 138:2, the psalmist wrote, "I will worship toward Your holy temple, and praise Your name for Your loving-kindness and for Your truth's sake; for You have magnified Your Word above all Your name" (MKJ). God takes His word seriously and if God makes a promise, His people can expect it to come to pass. However, carrying such a promise to completion can be as burden-laden as carrying a pregnancy full term.

You know the story; Abram and his wife Sarai (later named Sarah) had grown old and were child-less. When Abram was more than seventy-five years old, God promised that the number of his descendants would be as the stars in the sky. This promise came without a great deal of detail. God did not say when or how; He just said it would happen. Although Abram initially believed God, after being in the waiting room a number of years, he and Sarai began to talk about what God meant. It is always dangerous to try to interpret what God said without God's input. Sarai suggested that what God said was more complicated than it seemed. There would be descendants as God promised, but perhaps, while coming from Abram they would not come through her. It is amazing how often what God does in the spirit, seen by us in faith, is transformed into something else the longer we wait. This is what I call the "Cloning of God's Promise." Cloning the promise of God is when a person receives a promise from God then, for whatever reason, gets so involved in the process that what is produced, while being presented as the answered promise, is not neither can it ever be. At best, it is a mere facsimile or clone.

Technically speaking, Ishmael, who was born after the promise was made, was Abraham's son and heir to all he owned. Nevertheless, he was not the promise. The promise would come because of the miraculous intervention of God and not the rational interpretation and action of humans.

In today's medical world, cloning involves altering cells, reprogramming DNA and the stimulation of cell division. The result is that, through cloning, what is created is a genetic replica of something or someone. This does not mean that the clone is the original but that it has the potential to become like the original and the potential to do what the original can do. In this sense, Ishmael is a failed attempt to clone the promise of God. What Abram and Sarai tried to do may have been logical; it may have been noble, but it was not the plan or promise of God. Sarai and Abram were so caught up with the ends that they failed to see that in God's sight it is often all about the means. God promised Abram a male child who would inherit from Abram the promise and then pass on the inheritance to his children and their children. Perhaps to Abram and Sarai whether the child came through Sarai or Hagar was mere semantics. However, for God it was part of a divinely ordered plan, set forth before the foundations of the world. Although He does not say it until Gen 19:13, in God's heart and mind, the details of the promise were already laid out: "Then God said, 'Yes, but your wife Sarah will bear you a son, and you will call him Isaac. I will establish my covenant with him as an everlasting covenant for his descendants after him.'"

Abram, with Hagar, created a male child named Ishmael. When God makes a promise, whether He says it or not, to Him it is very specific. When we take hold of a situation, perhaps in an effort to help God, the best we can do is produce a clone of what God has in His heart. The best we can do is try to mimic the creative process that God alone controls. The clone may appear to be everything God promised in the beginning but as time goes on it will inevitably prove it is not the promise. For whatever similarities Ishmael and Isaac had, Ishmael was not Isaac. The promise that would echo throughout generations was not to Abraham and his first male son. It was to Abraham and the son God promised. It was not to the child of presumption but the child of promise. More frequently than we care to confess, we presume God means something and go for it full throttle only to be disappointed to know that God will not receive or accept what we have produced. God may bless it and may use it for our sakes but will not allow us to be deceived into believing or to deceive others into believing it is the promise. As much as it pains me to say, there are many people working jobs, ministering in churches, and living out marriages who have entered into relationships with clones. Some of these people are frustrated but tolerate the relationship. Others are content but live with the sense that something is missing. Granted a few have the right one at the wrong time, many others have welcomed Ishmael and have stopped waiting for Isaac. As a result, they will never realize the fulfillment that God desired and promised concerning their lives.

While some have contended that a clone is better than nothing at all, I pray you will see the danger in this type of thinking. The blessing that was incorporated in the promise was to flow through Isaac. If there was no Isaac where would the blessing be applied? Nowhere! There are generations lined up in the heart of God awaiting the fulfillment of what God has promised us.

Section Five

Promise Fulfilled!

"For all the promises of God find their Yes in him. That is why we utter the Amen through him, to the glory of God" (2 Cor. 1:20).

13

Our Season, God's Sovereignty

In Colossians 2:8 the apostle Paul writes, "See to it that no one takes you captive through hollow and deceptive philosophy, which depends on human tradition and the basic principles of this world rather than on Christ." If we are not careful, it is easy for us to get caught up in the worldly traditions. If we live our lives based on the trends or traditions of the world, we will find it very difficult to discern our individual seasons. After years of serving in ministry and working as a college counselor, I cannot tell you how many times I have talked with people who feel their lives should be further along than they are. After reading certain magazines, watching certain television programs or even the nightly news, you might begin to think that by age thirty, you are supposed to be married with a child. At thirty-two, you are supposed to have a new car. By thirty-five, you are supposed to have a house with a white picket fence, 3.2 children and a dog that does tricks. That's worldly tradition. Just because it is the ideal life for some, does not mean that it is the will of God for you. So what if you are forty years old and not married? Maybe God wanted to save you from ten years of misery. Many, who are divorced today, if asked, would say, "I should have waited." But how could you? Your friends were all married, your parents wanted grandchildren and marriage was the "end all" or at least that was the impression you got from the preacher and other members at church. Some of you who are remarried would probably say, "I should have just waited those extra years for this second person." If we are going to be honest, so many can say, "He beat me. She cheated. He walked out on the kids and me. She did drugs. If I had it to do over again, I would scratch those ten years and just wait for whoever God has for me." That is, if we would be honest. Yet, look around you, listen to the conversations, or listen to yourself. People are running around asking, "So and so has it, him, or her, when's my turn?"

God warns us not to be caught up in tradition. Our lives should not be patterned after trends but Christ and His will for us. We have been made complete in Christ. Anything God has for you will be in Christ. Perhaps you can relate. When you ask her if she is ready to go to church and she says, "I don't feel like going," you are confused because she felt like going just before you got married. After having performed a decent number of wedding ceremonies, regrettably, too often I hear how people have changed after the honeymoon (some after the wedding). I hesitate to tell you how many times Dr. Jekyll shows up for pre-marital counseling and Mr. Hyde leaves the church after the wedding. Wait on God! Have you watched the news or read a paper lately? Some of the finest, richest, most talented actors in Hollywood are also some of the most dysfunctional people in the country. Wait on God! He knows who they really are today and who they will be when their potion wears off — or once you marry them, ordain them, or accept their invitation to become their pastor. All you need is in Christ. If it is not in Christ, you do not need it.

To say that we should wait on God does not invalidate the question, "When is it my turn?" Although it probably would have felt better to write this book without having to live it, God required and continues to require me to wait for the fulfillment of promises just like the rest of His children. I do not mind waiting my turn. Still, it is a part of human nature to want to know when that turn will come. Unfortunately, none of my calendars has a date circled with the words, "My Turn" written next to it. The best I have found, through prayer and the scriptures, is that my turn comes at the time God has appointed for me. Your turn comes during the time or season God has appointed for you. Throughout history as God's people have awaited fulfillment of His promises, God simply has not been in the habit of giving out specific dates and times. Abraham did not know Jesus would come thousands of years after he died. But Jesus was the ultimate fulfillment of the promise. Abraham did not know when. God is just like that. Often we are given our marching orders with the footnote that we will be blessed and be a blessing - that's all! This is the will of God.

When I was 15 years old my elder brother Andre' graduated from high school. No problem. I did not expect to graduate that year. It would have clearly been out of order. As bright as I was, no one expected me to graduate 2 years early. My only expectation during that June ceremony was to rejoice with my brother and, with great pride, celebrate his achievement. How much easier it is when we know our season!

When a child is born in his or her God-appointed season it is a wonderful thing to behold and the scripture is more real to us than at any other time in our lives: "I have seen the burden God has laid on men. He has made everything beautiful in its time. He has also set eternity in the hearts of men; yet they cannot fathom what God has done from beginning to end" (Eccles. 3:10-11). As beautiful as a newborn baby is (or the fulfillment of any of God's promises), the burden is that it comes "in its time." But when it does come, it is beautiful! The hymn writer, Diana Bell, put it this way, "In His time, in His time; He makes all things beautiful in His time. Lord, please show me ev'ry day as You're teaching me Your way, that You do just what You say in Your time."

During the most transitional times of my life, I have found that when I waited for, depended on, and desperately needed the provision of God, God showed up when and how He wanted. I wanted God to show up on Monday with a ministry assignment and a large honorarium. God showed up on Friday with a check from a family member. I wanted God to show up with a new job that would enable me to buy food or clothing. Instead, God showed up with a meal prepared by a sister in Christ or a nice suit that someone from church could no longer wear. It is easy to become ungrateful for God's provision and blessings and, perhaps, even fail to recognize it is God who has provided and blessed, if we do not understand that God keeps his promises in our season, His way!

14

The Season of Fulfillment

What we consider the act of God fulfilling His promise is often much more than an act, it is a season. This Season of fulfillment often has several very specific characteristics. First, as was mentioned earlier, it comes in God's own sovereign time — what the Apostle Paul called "the fullness of time."

> Now what I am saying is this: As long as an heir is a child, he is no better off than a slave, even though he owns everything. Instead, he is placed under the control of guardians and trustees until the time set by the father. It was the same way with us. While we were children, we were slaves to the basic principles of the world. But when the fullness of time had come, God sent his Son, born of a woman, born under the law, in order to redeem those who were under the law, so that we might

receive adoption as his children. (Gal. 4:1-5 ISV)

Secondly, the season is simply that, a season. When it is summer, you expect it to be warm or hot, depending on where you live. When it is winter, you expect snow or at least colder weather, depending on where you live. At the same time, within the season of winter there will be some days which resemble spring. In the season of summer, there will be some days that resemble spring or even fall. It is the same when it comes to the season of fulfillment. God's presence and blessings may be evident. Yet there will be some days that resemble the previous season from which God has just brought us. Without spending too much time elaborating on this point, I believe it is worth noting that as the Hebrews left Egypt and found Pharaoh's army closing in and the Red Sea in front of them, some said to Moses, "Didn't we say to you in Egypt, 'Leave us alone; let us serve the Egyptians?' It would have been better for us to serve the Egyptians than to die in the desert!'" To paraphrase, they were saying, "We told you before this cannot be the season of fulfillment and now we are going to die." (Exod. 14:9-12) They had been in bondage for so long and when their way of escape seemed blocked, they assumed they were heading back to a life of bondage. However, when God says it is time, no military force or force of nature can hinder you from receiving the deliverance, healing, and other things He has promised. Stand still and see the salvation of the Lord!

This brings us to the third point. When the season of fulfillment comes, it must be embraced by faith. On numerous occasions, the Hebrews wanted to throw their hands up and return to Egypt. Maybe they thought they were being set up or had just miscalculated God's plan and timing. In fact, when the Hebrews finally reached the brink of the Promised Land and sent twelve in to spy it out, ten of the twelve spies reported that, in essence, the people had missed God and could not take the land (Exod. chapters 13 & 14). It takes faith not to turn back and it takes faith to press forward when circumstances, and even loved ones, call into question what season you are really in now.

Did I mention that the Season of Fulfillment will have obstacles, trials, and tribulations, just like any other season? Unfortunately, even greater ones than those you have already experienced! Moses stood and prophesied to the people at the Red Sea, "Do not be afraid. Stand firm and you will see the deliverance the Lord will bring you today. The Egyptians you see today you will never see again" (14:13). However, what God did not give Moses to share with the people is that their precious Promised Land was filled with Canaanites, Amorites, Hittites, Perizzites, Hivites and the Jebusites. In the season of fulfillment, it is good to remember the words of the Rev. James Cleveland: "Nobody told me that the road would be easy but I don't believe He brought me this far to leave me."

If the season of promise can have some of the same problems we might expect in any other season, how will we recognize it? Perhaps what we will see first is the "milk and honey." This term means very little to a people living in the 21st century who can walk into just about any grocery store or corner store and find milk and honey. However, the biblical phrase "milk and honey" was "a proverbial expression, abounding with the choicest fruits, both for necessity and delight" (Exod. 3:8, John Wesley's Explanatory Notes on the Whole Bible 1754-1765). The season of fulfillment is one in which, despite the presence of negative circumstances and situations, God keeps bringing what is enjoyable and beneficial to you.

Your job may not pay six figures, your spouse may not look like a supermodel or superman, and your house may not have six bedrooms and six bathrooms. Yet what you have is still a blessing to you and still beneficial.

Next, seasons come via a process. Be careful when your dream man or woman wants to marry you but does not want premarital counseling. Be careful when people want to be ordained before being licensed or receive a doctorate prior to receiving a bachelors or masters degree.

Lastly, despite what you see or hear, often like most of the extremely precious gifts from God, the season of fulfillment is discerned. Just because we do not see it with our eyes, hear it with our ears, or even fathom it with our minds does not mean the very season we await is not upon us. "However, as it is written: 'No eye has seen, no ear has heard, no mind has conceived what God has prepared for those who love him but God has revealed it to us by his Spirit.

The Spirit searches all things, even the deep things of God" (1 Cor. 2:9-10).

God is able to speak to our hearts or simply allow us to discern the shift from one season to the next before we see any change at all. Just as we can sense the seasons of the year changing before the calendar declares a new one, if we are sensitive to God, God will allow each of us to sense his or her season arriving while we await its time of fulfillment.

15

Promises Fulfilled

As with most preachers, I find it difficult not to declare what God has done in my life. Although the promises we anticipate from God may be as diverse as the seasons in which they will arrive, each of us can or will be able to declare God's faithfulness and point to fulfilled promises. Here are a few of mine …

Promise of love

As far back as I can remember, I have always yearned for intimate relationships as opposed to superficial exchanges. While others wanted autographs and pictures of celebrities, I wanted to have meaningful conversation with them. When many of my friends wanted fleeting moments of lust, I longed for lasting love. While some wanted a person to share their homes with, I wanted someone to spend my life with. For years, this desire went unfulfilled. It was not until I went away to college that, while on the campus of Lincoln University, God instilled in my heart that I knew my wife or was about to meet her. This knowing was as a promise and I held to it until it was fulfilled. I discovered that the person I met only months before leaving for college, who had grown to be one of my best friends, was destined to be my wife. It took two years of friendship, six months of dating, six months of engagement and the promise was fulfilled in a moment.

Promise of Ministry

Over the years, I have met and ministered to people who came to Christ just after hitting rock bottom. Shattered dreams, broken hearts, various addictions and persecutions drove them to the end of themselves. There they met Jesus and began the most life-altering relationship imaginable. This was not my testimony. I was raised in a traditional Baptist church and it was not the fear of hell that drew me to Christ. It was the promise of ministry or, more precisely, the promise of purpose. I came to God because, despite my relatively content life, I sensed God calling me to so much more. As Stephen Hurd sings, "Zion, is calling me to a higher place of praise!" I felt God calling me to a place where He could be praised and glorified through what I said, how I lived, who I became. This calling, and even promise, to use me if I would commit my life to Him was fulfilled as I served God and people as a man of God, an associate minister, then youth pastor, then senior pastor, then interim pastor, traveling minister, writer and even in the secular realm as college counselor.

Promise of Home and Community

When I was in seminary, I recall a season where I was infatuated with houses. Everywhere I went I eyed the homes and even took pictures. One day I heard God speak to my heart, "Don't worry about your house. It's taken care of." From that moment, I stopped looking. Just prior to Lisa and I purchasing our first, second and third homes we did quite a bit a looking. However, each of the homes came miraculously and none came through our diligent searching.

In 2005, the interim governor of New Jersey began a contest to find a new slogan for the state. Although I had already moved to Ohio I felt compelled to send in what I am sure is the greatest slogan ever: "New Jersey, All You Want in A State and More." It did not win. I love New Jersey and am so proud to be from a state that has such a great diversity of people, places and things. Simultaneously, I recognize that for much of my adulthood I did not seem to fit in. I do not mind waiting ten to fifteen seconds after the traffic light turns green before I lay on the horn. I do not mind saying good morning to any stranger who happens to look me in the eye. I do not even mind telling the person at Wal-Mart about a moment in my day or life while the cashier waits for a manager to sign off on an over-ring. I have come to realize that some of the things that drive people crazy in the North East don't bother me much. We are finding the slower paced life, in a community that seems to emphasize some of the courtesies found less in larger cities, to be extremely addictive. None of this came to mind when God began to impress on my heart to leave the pastorate of Grace Baptist Church and move to Steubenville, OH. Yet, having arrived, interacted with the natives, and purchased our dream home, I can see God's promise for a safe and nurturing home and community environment being fulfilled — perhaps I should say, "yet again!"

The Promise I Never Heard

In attempting to convey what I mean by "A promise I never heard," I have to talk about my paternal grandmother. In my spirit, I seem to know, as though I actually heard God say it, that the grief she experienced because of some in her family, would be overshadowed by the fulfillment of this promise: that God would draw the members of her family to Him. Perhaps when I get to heaven I'll find out if I was completely wrong or right on target but, here is the picture. As a child, I was blessed to grow up near three of my four grandparents. I spent more time with my maternal grandmother, Emily Brown. She was the perfect image of "Grandma" - loving, firm, nurturing. Yet, for some reason, I felt extremely close to my father's mother, my Nana, Olive Foster – perhaps because our birthdays were so close. My memories of her are few and most of them would be relatively insignificant to the average person. Still, some of those moments were life defining for me. My Nana was diagnosed with cancer when I was a teenager. After what sometimes seemed like years and at other times only a few days, it became apparent that my Nana was not going to live. I vividly recall praying, "Lord, don't take her, take me." Needless to say, the answer to that prayer was "No." I did not hear a response but I kept living and my Nana went home to be with the Lord. Today, I long to hear the promise that kept me here. Today, I long to hear the promise that kept me from AIDS, from having children outside of marriage, from prison, from living a life laced with trinkets but with little eternal value. This early morning as I write these thoughts I do so with tears in my eyes because I believe the outcome of my life is the fulfillment of a promise God made to my Nana. I long to hear the actual promise that did not keep me from a reckless life but kept that reckless life from wrecking my destiny in God. I believe the promise may have sounded like this, "Olive, I know some of your children did not turn out the way you planned or prayed. I know sometimes it's hard to see me working in their lives and sometimes they break your heart. Olive, I am bigger than what you see right now. Even from those that seem so far from me, I will raise up a generation that will love me, honor me, live for me and tell the world about me. Olive, like Abraham and Sarah, you will see the beginning of what I do from earth, the rest you will see from the banisters of glory. Trust me. I fulfill my promises."

There is an interesting scripture in 2 Kings chapter 13 that reads, "Hazael king of Aram oppressed Israel throughout the reign of Jehoahaz. But the Lord was gracious to them and had compassion and showed concern for them because of his covenant with Abraham, Isaac and Jacob. To this day he has been unwilling to destroy them or banish them from his presence" (2 Kings 13:22-23).

I am almost certain, that the grace-filled relationship I enjoy with God and the blessed life I am privileged to live today has very much to do with the fulfillment of a promise God made to my great grandparents, my grandparents and, especially my Nana, even before I was born.

16

Just Wanted To Say Thanks

It is a wonderful thing when a man or woman can sing with Rev. Clay Evans, "When I look back over my life and I think things over, I can truly say that I've been blessed..." Without question this song articulates the summary of my findings when I consider where I have been and the miraculous way the Lord has brought me to where I am. At the same time, my life has been laced with challenges, disappointments and even a number of embarrassments. I have been responsible for the greatest embarrassments. Still, there are a few embarrassments that seemed to grow from seeds I did not plant. One year, we threw a birthday party at the church for one of my sons. It was not a major event as far as major events go. A few of his friends got together and put on costumes my wife Lisa made for them. That year's theme was Buzz Lightyear. Everything was going well - no injuries, no fights, and no major damage to church property. Then it was time to open the gifts. I feared that my darling son might not show equal appreciation for every gift he received. To my surprise, other than the clothes he received from one of his godmothers he expressed the same amount of enthusiasm for each gift. Every gift he received was special to him - for about three seconds. I was so embarrassed. Before he could get all of the wrapping paper off of one gift, he seemed to be reaching for the next one. This is not how we had raised him. Where did this come from? What I have come to realize is that some things are taught while other things are caught. Such displays of ingratitude do not need to be taught, they are a part of our nature. We do not mean to be ungrateful, we just are. Having received what we have long awaited from God, we must not simply launch out on the next quest or start bombarding God with new petitions before we say "Thank You!"

In his gospel, Luke records an encounter Jesus had with ten lepers:

> As he was going into a village, ten men who had leprosy met him. They stood at a distance and called out in a loud voice, "Jesus, Master, have pity on us!" When he saw them, he said, "Go, show yourselves to the priests." And as they went, they were cleansed. One of them, when he saw he was healed, came back, praising God in a loud voice. He threw himself at Jesus' feet and thanked him—and he was a Samaritan. Jesus asked, "Were not all ten cleansed? Where are the other nine?

Was no one found to return and give praise to
God except this foreigner?" Then he said to
him, "Rise and go; your faith has made you
well."

Upon hearing that Jesus was coming into the city,
ten lepers stood at a distance and shouted for mercy.
Jesus instructed them to go and show themselves to
the priests. While clearly still plagued with leprosy,
the ten set out in faith and were healed as they went.
Far too often, we want to see the conclusion of the
matter before we do what God said. How many times
has God said, "Give" but we did not because we did
not see how we were going to meet some other obligation? How many times has God said, "Go speak"
but because we did not know in advance what we
would say we did not go? Often, it is the faith-filled
act of obedience that leads to the blessings of God.

In this account, nine of the lepers received their
healing and went about their business. However,
"one of them, when he saw he was healed, came
back, praising God in a loud voice. He threw himself
at Jesus' feet and thanked him—and he was a
Samaritan" (Luke 17:15-16).

This man was instructed by Jesus to go to the
priest. This man had a life to reclaim. Perhaps he had
a family he had not seen or provided for since the
leprous outbreak. Furthermore, I am sure he, like the
others, had news he couldn't keep to himself. Still,
the Bible says the Samaritan returned to Jesus and
said, in essence, "I just wanted to say 'Thanks!'"

This is the second time in the Gospel of Luke that a Samaritan's character exceeded that of those who considered themselves the people of God. It is a Samaritan that is a neighbor to the fallen sojourner in chapter ten and it is the Samaritan who goes back to say "Thanks" for his healing. How interesting! Perhaps there is a lesson in humility to be learned from these accounts. When those deemed unworthy of the blessings of God receive them, it is not a strange thing for them to say, "Thank you!"

While the Faith movement did much to encourage the Church to believe God for what seemed to be impossible, it also did a lot of harm. Many Christians, rather than having faith in God, seemed to have faith in faith. The question was not if one knew God well enough to trust God, but rather, if one had the faith to get what he or she wanted from God. The book of Hebrews teaches us "And without faith it is impossible to please God, because anyone who comes to him must believe that he exists and that he rewards those who earnestly seek him" (11:6). Faith really is about who God is, our quest to know Him and what it requires to please Him, rather than if we have what it takes to control God. What is amazing is that once *we* have concluded that *we* have enough faith to get God to act, we then believe that, based on that faith, God is *obligated* to act. While we wear masks of humility like the other nine lepers who also cried for mercy, often our hearts prayer is, "My kingdom come, my will be done, in heaven as it is on earth." How arrogant! This was one of the scariest things about the Faith movement— its arrogance. Instead of humbly submitting ourselves to the will of God and being thankful for what He does, we act as if, because God is our Heavenly Father, He owes us or we deserve it. If we feel we deserve or have somehow earned what God graciously does for us, we are not far from being able to go about our lives without so much as a "Thank you."

In Deuteronomy chapter nine, God is speaking to the people about entering into Canaan. He gives the people a warning, perhaps to prevent the arrogance we see in the New Testament Pharisees and others who thought they enjoyed the favor of God because of their good works. God tells them,

> After the Lord your God has driven them out before you, do not say to yourself, "The Lord has brought me here to take possession of this land because of my righteousness." No, it is on account of the wickedness of these nations that the Lord is going to drive them out before you. It is not because of your righteousness or your integrity that you are going in to take possession of their land; but on account of the wickedness of these nations, the Lord your God will drive them out before you, to accomplish what he swore to your fathers, to Abraham, Isaac and Jacob (Deut. 9:4-5).

Jim Carey starred in a movie titled *Bruce Almighty* (Universal Pictures, 2002). Without question Jim Carey is one of my least favorite comedians and some of the films he has starred in should have been burned prior to their release. When the previews for *Bruce Almighty* began to run on television I was appalled. "How dare he! How dare they!" I questioned. It was certainly a change of pace to see Morgan Freeman as God - considering his ethnicity and former roles. Still my curiosity could not overcome my righteous indignation of a carnal, ungodly, lust-filled human allowed to possess God's power and misuse it for his own purposes. Revelation! It happens every Sunday in many Jesus-loving, Bible teaching, churches around the world. While on vacation one year, I was flipping through the channels and came across this movie. I recalled hearing someone say that the commercials did not properly convey the true intent of the movie or the message it sought to get across. I watched. Hmmm. I watched some more. Before I knew it, the movie was going off. The message the movie sought to express was made clearest in Jim Carey's cry to God in the last ten minutes or so of the movie, "I surrender. Whatever you want to do with my life is o.k." Although Jim Carey's character as seen in the earlier parts of the movie was an extreme mess, it is easy to see where many of us, with the same powers would use them for similar purposes. In fact, this is exactly why certain prayers go unanswered and certain desires go unfulfilled. James wrote, "You want something but don't get it. You kill and covet, but you cannot have what you want. You quarrel and fight. You do not have, because you do not ask God. When you ask, you do not receive, because you ask with wrong motives, that you may spend what you get on your pleasures" (James 4:2-3). God does not owe us and the purpose of our lives is not about us, it is about God.

As a minister, I often get the opportunity to eat out with all types of people. Unfortunately, some of the people with whom I have dined clearly had classist attitudes towards those serving us. They remind me of the arrogant, stuck-up snobs one might read about in novels or see in the movies where the butler, maid and chauffer serve them whole-heartedly and they just take it all in. Like a king or queen on a throne, they barely acknowledge the servants, let alone express any degree of gratitude. God does not exist to serve at our pleasure but we at His. Therefore, we should be grateful for every prayer answered, every door opened, and every breath taken. Kurt Carr states it beautifully in the song, *For Every Mountain*, "For every mountain You brought me over, for every trial you've seen me through, for every blessing, Hallelujah, for this I give You praise."

While no leper was worthy of an audience with Jesus, it was a foreigner, the least worthy among them, who returned not to ask for something else, but just to say, "Thank You!" Did the others, those who were the "seed of Abraham," think they deserved to be healed? While the gentiles worry about their most basic needs, our Heavenly Father knows what we need (Matt. 6:32). Is it because we belong to God and call God "Father" that we do not feel compelled to express gratitude as we should? Has familiarity indeed bred contempt? Do we feel "Why should we thank God for keeping a promise - especially when it took so long for Him to do so?"

Some have presented our relationship with God and our privilege to use the name of Jesus as though it afforded us certain inalienable rights. Therefore, if we "named it" we could "claim it." I have heard it said, "If you .... God has to ..." John the Baptist told the Pharisees, "Produce fruit in keeping with repentance. And do not think you can say to your-selves, 'We have Abraham as our father.' I tell you that out of these stones God can raise up children for Abraham" (Matt. 3:8-9). We do not have the right to think because we are children of God, God owes us anything or must do what we request. I sincerely believe this type of thinking causes us to be so unthankful.

Psalm 100 is one of the most famous of the psalms for good reason. It contains only five verses. Four of the five verses tell the reader how to respond to God. Verse three tells us why. When we know and remember that "the Lord is God. It is He who made us, and we are his; we are His people, the sheep of His pasture (v.3)" it only makes sense to "Enter his gates with thanksgiving and his courts with praise; give thanks to him and praise his name" (v.4). It is not God who owes us anything. We owe God everything.

Ingratitude is such an unacceptable response to God's provision and blessing that the absence of the remaining nine lepers at the thanksgiving service drew the sarcasm of Jesus. "Jesus asked, 'were not all ten cleansed? Where are the other nine'" (Luke 17:17)? Having somewhat of a sarcastic nature myself, if I were Jesus I would have said something like, "Only one of the ten got healed? That's only ten percent! I must be having an off day!" or "Hmm, make a mental note, 'inform lepers that it is o.k. to return to express appreciation prior to going to see priest.'"

Let me say a brief word about sin as it relates to gratitude and do let me be graphic in my illustration of the point. The devil will always desire to cause us to sin after God heals, delivers, provides or blesses. When we give in to a temptation and sin after God blesses us it is like a young man home from college, sitting at the dinner table, and his mother brings him a plate full of all of his favorite foods - made the way that only Momma could make them. As he tastes the food, everything in him wants to sit in that moment forever and enjoy each bite over and over again. Just as he finishes desert he says, "Mom, you have outdone yourself! The food was better than it had ever been! Thank you so much!" Then he spits in her face. Graphic, but this young man's conduct understates the disrespect we show God when we consider who God is and all that God has done for us!

It is unlikely that too much can ever be said or written on the topic of gratitude. Each of us has experienced ingratitude from children, spouses, bosses, friends and others. If we consider our own feelings during those moments when others appeared ungrateful, and factor in the sovereignty of God as found in Psalm One Hundred, we will be far more grateful in the future and far more intentional about expressing our gratitude.

17

A Time for Dancing

When a woman is pregnant, prior to the child's birth, there is a celebration. Although the event is designed to provide what the baby needs, make no mistake about it, it is a party. When a man and woman prepare for marriage, it is customary for friends and relatives to throw numerous parties for them. The engagement party, bachelor and bachelorette parties, bridal shower, and even the wedding reception given by the bride and groom after the wedding are all events to celebrate the fulfillment of God's promise to the man and woman. When these events are holy, they glorify God and they are much like the many celebrations we find in Jewish tradition. As I consider the roots of Christianity, it amazes me how far some of our churches have gotten from our Jewish heritage. For some, church is dry and boring, almost lifeless. Very much unlike the celebratory time in the presence of God that we find in many Old

Testament passages. The Jewish people have always been a celebrating people. In fact, a Jewish wedding consisted of seven days of celebration.

Time and again, we wait for God and wait for God and, when God comes through, we whimper out a "Thank you" and fall asleep. I remember when I got married. It was a miracle! As I mentioned earlier, I left college thinking Lisa and I might get married in three years or perhaps one year. One night while we were walking and talking I sensed that God was moving up the time. Lisa sensed the same thing. Actually, God was not moving up the time, He was moving us into the time He had already set. God does not change our "due date." He simply allows us to know that we are further along than we thought. Within a matter of weeks we were planning the wedding and that coming August we were married. Although we asked my sister to coordinate, because of my hands-on, extremely particular way of doing things, we were running like mad people the week prior to the wedding. In fact, the day of the wedding, twice I drove some two and a half hours to Pennsylvania to pick up food for the reception. By the time of the ceremony, we were both exhausted. So often, the wait seems so long and the work so hard that when God comes through we are too tired to dance. However, we must remember that this is indeed the moment for which we have been waiting - and celebrate!

A common scenario, especially among bishops and pastors, is to spend the first ten minutes of service celebrating the fulfillment of God's promise and the next hour preaching about where we are going next. Before the ribbon is cut on the first building, we are spying out the land for the next building. Before the chicken is digested from the dinner celebrating the first church plant, we are asking God where to plant the next church. Sometimes we can barely get across the Red Sea before we are planning our entrance into Canaan. However, the Bible tells us that upon crossing the Red Sea, "Then Miriam the prophetess, Aaron's sister, took a tambourine in her hand, and all the women followed her, with tambourines and dancing" (Exod. 15:20). They celebrated! Even Solomon, as busy as he must have been sharing wisdom and amassing wealth, understood that there is "a time to dance." (Eccles. 3:4)

One of the least dignified moments in King David's life and ministry occurred when the Ark of the Covenant was returned. The ark had been captured by the Philistines after the battle where Eli's sons Hophni and Phinehas were killed (1 Sam. 4:11). The Philistines possessed it for seven months, then, following the death of Uzza, it was in the house of Obed-edom for an additional three moths. For nearly a year, the Ark of the Covenant had been away from Israel.

Now King David was told, "The Lord has blessed the household of Obed-Edom and everything he has, because of the ark of God." So David went down and brought up the ark of God from the house of Obed-Edom to the City of David with rejoicing. When those who were carrying the ark of the Lord had taken six steps, he sacrificed a bull and a fattened calf. David, wearing a linen ephod, danced before the Lord with all his might, while he and the entire house of Israel brought up the ark of the Lord with shouts and the sound of trumpets. (2 Sam. 6:12-15)

This type of celebration was typical for the return of troops from battle, loved ones from long journeys and even wayward children who came home. Jesus speaks of the rejoicing that occurs when something valuable is found after having been lost - a lost coin, a lost sheep and, especially, a lost child (Luke 15). How much more should we rejoice when God pays off the student loan or mortgage, when God heals us of an illness, when God saves our loved one?

If we stop for a minute and think about what it took for God to bring the promise He made to us to pass, shouting, dancing, celebrating would seem less of an option. God had to send funds, move on the hearts of decision makers, not to mention, God had to transform us into people He could use. Do you remember the Moses God confronted on the back-side of the Mountain? This Moses was unwilling to go to Egypt with God alone (Exod. chapters 3&4). However, by Exodus 33:15 his prayer to God was, "If your Presence does not go with us, do not send us up from here." From the time of promise to the time of fulfillment, Moses underwent an amazing trans-formation. If we simply recall who we were when we started the journey and then look in the mirror on the day of fulfillment, that alone is enough to cause us to nearly lose our minds in praise and celebration!

Let me say one more thing on this topic. Don't be too tired to praise Him. The sleepless nights, the constant arguing with your spouse, the endless phone calls from bill collectors, having to work two or three jobs — so many things in the waiting room have sought to drain the very life out of you. As you press your way through the darkness and into the light, you want to just fall down and sleep. However, you have been waiting on God and He has promised that you would receive new strength. Lay hold of some of that new strength and use it to praise God! When Miriam danced, she was both celebrating what had been done but also praising the One who did it. David was not merely celebrating that the Ark was being returned; he was also praising the God who allowed Him to retrieve it and bring it back to Israel. Do not be so tired from the journey that you fail to celebrate and give God the praise due Him.

18

Couldn't Keep it to Myself

One day our son Vaughn and I were watching an old episode of *Bugs Bunny*. In this particular episode, Bugs and Daffy were trying to get to Myrtle Beach but made the wrong turn at Albuquerque. When they emerged from their underground tunnel, they found themselves in a cave. While Bugs reviewed the map in an attempt to find out where they went wrong and how to get back on course, Daffy stood spellbound. What had caught Daffy's attention in such a mesmerizing way was gold, silver and various kinds of precious stones. Completely unaware of Daffy's discovery Bugs continued to study the map. Without sign or warning, Daffy pounced on Bugs' head and began to jump up and down until Bugs was completely submerged under the dirt. Daffy's proclamation: "It's mine, mine, all mine!"

While this very well may be the cry of many who experience some degree of prosperity or wealth, most people when receiving good news or some kind of blessing seek to share the good news with someone. In fact, those who determine they will not share the good news of their situation with others find themselves battling an almost invincible foe. Like actors in a popular commercial advertising medication to lower one's cholesterol, many people who experience the fulfillment of long awaited promises find themselves telling both friends and strangers of the blessing they received. Many of these people do it not because the news will bless or change the lives of others but because they simply cannot keep it to themselves.

Perhaps you will recall the leper of Mark chapter one. In this passage, a man with leprosy approached Jesus and pleaded with him. The scripture records that he "begged him on his knees, 'If you are willing, you can make me clean'" (v.40). According to Leviticus 13, the man should have met with Jesus outside of the city. In fact, he was to live alone outside of the city, his clothes were to be torn, his head shaved, his upper lip covered and he was to cry, "Unclean! Unclean!" This man viewed Jesus through eyes of faith. In return, Jesus viewed the man, not through the eyes of public opinion or the law but through eyes of mercy. "Filled with compassion, Jesus reached out his hand and touched the man. 'I am willing,' he said. 'Be clean!' Immediately the leprosy left him and he was cured" (vv. 40-42).

Jesus does not send the man to the priest so that he could determine *if* the man was cleansed; he told him to offer the sacrifice required of one who *was* cleansed. Within his stern charge, Jesus instructed the man not to say anything to anyone. One would think that this man, having been relieved of his discomfort and disgrace, would follow what Jesus said to the letter. "But when the man left, he began to proclaim it freely. He spread the word so widely that Jesus could no longer enter a town openly, but had to stay out in deserted places..." (v. 45 ISV).

Albeit this man's blatant disobedience appears to have complicated matters for Jesus in his ministry to those in need, the scriptures never state that he lost his healing or was in any way penalized for spreading the word. Perhaps it was because God understood that the man, as much as he may have wanted, couldn't keep it to himself.

The Samaritan woman of John chapter four introduced Jesus to her entire town because after speaking with Jesus and learning who he was, she couldn't keep it to herself. The man called Legion in Mark 5 wanted to follow Jesus after he had been delivered from many demons. However, without a seminary education or a ministerial license, Jesus instructs him to begin his public ministry by telling others what the Lord had done for him. How easy it must have been for this man to follow this command. The reality is Jesus did not need someone with this man's testimony hanging around sharing his testimony. The people encountering Jesus would gain their own testimonies. Those who had not met Jesus were the ones who needed to hear this man's story. They were the ones who needed to hear of the great things the Lord had done for him. Certainly, there are those who come to church whose faith is increased by hearing how God has saved, healed, delivered and made a way. Nevertheless, how much more those outside of the house of God need to know that, like the hymn proclaims, "to the utmost, Jesus saves ... He will pick you up and turn you around, Hallelujah! Jesus saves!"

Too many well-meaning church folk expect the church to grow based on the efforts of the pastor. Yet, throughout scripture we learn how "those who have been dug up by the plow shears of the Gospel" - as former generations would put it - have spread the word of their own transformation and a person, a family, a city, a region was saved. The slave girl in 2 Kings chapter 5, because of her compassion and concern for her mistress' husband, stated, "...If only my master would see the prophet who is in Samaria! He would cure him of his leprosy" (v. 3). While the King did not understand the power of God working through the man of God, this slave girl did. Because of her brief but powerful testimony, Naaman was healed and confessed, "Now I know that there is no God in all the world but in Israel" (v.15). The greatest books written are not theoretical in nature but experiential. One can think, imagine or wish a certain thing but it is when a person has seen, heard or experienced it that it has the power to change the lives of those who receive their testimony.

The song, *I Shall Wear a Crown* by Thomas A. Whitfield, proclaims that upon arriving in heaven, "I'm going to put on my robe, tell the story, how I made it over." However, we must not wait until we get to heaven. We must tell our story now! It is of paramount importance that we share with others the promise God made, how God met us in the waiting room, how God fulfilled His promise in ways we could have never imagined and how we were developed and changed through the process.

One day the Lord showed me something in Romans 8:28 that I had not seen before. "And we know that in all things God works for the good of those who love him, who have been called according to his purpose." For years, I have stood on, shouted on and depended on this scripture to bring me through certain trials. I knew that no matter what I faced, because I loved God and was "called according to His purpose," all things were working together for my good and God was working in all things for my good. Then I saw it, or heard it! "I am not the only one who loves God and is called according to His purpose." I realized that I would go through some things that would work together for the good of someone else who loves God and is called according to his purpose. I would go through some things and God would be at work in the midst of them for someone else's good. As I go through what I go through and share it with others, it works together for their good. Revelation 12:11 states, "They overcame him by the blood of the Lamb and by the word of their testimony; they did not love their lives so much as to shrink from death." I do not believe what is meant is simply that each person's testimony will cause him or her to overcome. It may mean this. However, it also may mean that your testimony will help me to overcome, my testimony will help you overcome and our testimonies will help someone else to overcome.

The Apostle Paul wrote to the church at Corinthians,

> Praise be to the God and Father of our Lord Jesus Christ, the Father of compassion and the God of all comfort, who comforts us in all our troubles, so that we can comfort those in any trouble with the comfort we ourselves have received from God. For just as the sufferings of Christ flow over into our lives, so also through Christ our comfort overflows. If we are distressed, it is for your comfort and salvation; if we are comforted, it is for your comfort, which produces in you patient endurance of the same sufferings we suffer. (2 Cor. 1:3-6)

One of the hardest situations I had ever faced in my life was when the Lord told me it was time to leave the pastorate of Grace Baptist Church. I vividly recall the season of my father's passing and preaching his eulogy. It was without question harder to leave the pastorate, the Ministers Council of NJ, and those who had become family to me in NJ than it was to preach that eulogy. Perhaps it is only as I write these words that I understand why this may have been. When my father died, everyone around me, family and friends, coworkers and acquaintances, the saved and unsaved, all knew what it was like to have someone they cared about pass away. The support and comfort was overwhelming. To date I cannot recall, as is often the case in these types of situations, anyone who should and could have been there who was not. However, as we prepared to undertake this major change in our lives, many of those who had enjoyed our company, appreciated our ministry, and who had not been asked to make similar sacrifices, did not, could not, or simply refused to understand. For all of the prophetic words that stated God was going to bless us and fulfill his plan for our lives, it seemed that no one expected He would do it in this way. Few, very few, were there to comfort and even fewer understood.

I recall one meeting at the church when we were planning what would take place after I was gone. One of the church leaders bluntly retorted, "What do you care, you are leaving?" What hurt most was that it was not my choice, but it was my season. I was not stepping out in faith; I was stepping out in obedience to the One on whom my faith was built. The day I was to announce to the congregation that I was leaving was the most difficult day in my life. Even as I took the pulpit, I prayed that if I was missing God, there would be a sign. There was a dramatic interruption as I began my sermon. An out-of-order parishioner delayed the moment but did not offer an out from God. I preached, "Stay in the Groove" inspired by the movie, *The Emperor's New Groove* (Walt Disney Feature Animation, 2000). I preached that Jesus had a groove, a pattern of life, that He lived and it was to do the Father's will. In like fashion, we ought to stay in the groove and do as God has called us to do. In my conclusion I announced that in order to "stay in the groove" I had to do what the Father said to do. In this case, it meant leaving. I am not sure if it was the best way to tell the people. I also do not know if I could have told them any other way.

With only a few prophetic voices around me and only a select number of people who truly seemed to understand this Abraham-like calling and response, I was determined but heart-broken. This particular year the *Eagle's Gathering*, an annual conference for ministers sponsored by Donald Hilliard Ministries, was to be held in North Carolina. Money was tight and my interest in going was nowhere near where it needed to be for me to make the journey. Two of my dearest friends, Thomas and Nadira Keaton, felt led to buy me a plane ticket. Now I had little choice; I was going. During one of the sessions, a pastor preached (and testified) about how God had called him from a place where things were going well and he was well-known to a place many thought was beneath him. I danced, I cried, I shouted! Not only was his testimony confirmation, it was affirmation. I had already heard from God and was poised to do exactly what I heard but this message came to affirm me in my decision. The entire chain of events was miraculous and I could have literally left the conference after he finished. I was there to hear that message. I do recall several other amazing messages from that gathering. However, as you might imagine, none impacted me like this brother's sharing his testimony. I am so glad he did not keep it to himself. What is God doing in your life? What has God done? The struggles, the successes, the failures, the joys, the heartbreaks, and even the embarrassments may very well be the testimony someone needs to hear to follow God or to keep their sanity while following God. Be discerning but whatever your story, tell someone. Don't keep it to yourself.

19

The Conclusion of the Matter

In Ecc 12:13, Solomon wrote, "Let us hear the conclusion of the whole matter. Fear God, and keep His commandments. For this *is* the whole *duty* of man." What a fitting way to wrap up! Here we have one deemed to be the wealthiest and wisest man who ever lived say, "It's not about me." As we wait on the Lord, we must not for a minute believe that the purpose of God's promise or God fulfilling His promise is all about us. As you will recall, the promise of promises, the one God made to Abram, was not only for Abram's benefit.

> And Jehovah said to Abram, Go out of your country, and from your kindred, and from your father's house into a land that I will show you. And I will make you a great nation. And I will bless you and make your name great. And you shall be a blessing. And I will bless

those that bless you and curse the one who curses you. And in you shall all families of the earth be blessed. (Gen. 12:1-3 MKJ)

As Abram responded to God's call to leave his own country in both faith and obedience, God promised to make him a great nation, bless him, and make his name great. However, God also promised to make him a blessing (presumably to other people) and to allow others to position themselves for blessings or curses depending on how they treated Abram. In addition, He says through Abram "all families of the earth" will be blessed or "bless themselves." God loves us, makes promises to us, and has a plan that includes us but the world does not revolve around us! The world revolves around God and His plan - for our lives AND the lives of others. The promise we so desperately want fulfilled incorporates promises God has made to others. As God fulfills His promise to us, He is at the very same time fulfilling His promise to countless others.

After a life showered with God's favor and blessing, a life of both faithfulness and idolatry, Solomon reminds us that the blessings of God and the fulfillment of every promise is related to our divinely ordained duty or calling; at the center of which is not our desire but God's. In the words of one of Charles Wesley's most renowned hymns, "A charge to keep I have, a God to glorify; a never-dying soul to save, and fit it for the sky. To serve this present age, my calling to fulfill, may it all my power engage, to do my Master's will."

Wherever you are in your season of waiting, know that you are not waiting in vain. God has a plan that will bless you and others. Despite the utter exhaustion you sometimes feel, remember the words of Isaiah:

> He giveth power to the faint; and to *them that have* no might he increaseth strength. Even the youths shall faint and be weary, and the young men shall utterly fall: But they that wait upon the Lord shall renew *their* strength; they shall mount up with wings as eagles; they shall run, and not be weary; *and* they shall walk, and not faint. (Isa. 40:29-31 KJV)

Know that your wait, like certain seasons of the year, may seem endless but must in its time give way to the season God has destined to follow - the season of fulfillment. Know that during your wait you will gain more and become more through the process of waiting than you could if the process had been averted. Know that your pain, your struggle, your wait, is redemptive for both you and for others. Know that as long as you are waiting for the God of Abraham and Sarah, Elijah and Esther, Solomon and the apostles, as long as you are waiting for Yahweh, your wait is for a God worth waiting for!

Printed in the United States
130216LV00001B/1-150/P

9 781606 478295